Infant/Toddler Caregiving

A Guide to

Social-Emotional Growth and Socialization

Edited by J. Ronald Lally

Developed by the

Center for Child and Family Studies

Far West Laboratory for Educational Research and Development

for the

Child Development Division

California Department of Education

the **Program** for infant toddler caregivers

Publishing Information

Infant/Toddler Caregiving: A Guide to Social-Emotional Growth and Socialization was developed by the Center for Child and Family Studies, Far West Laboratory for Educational Research and Development, San Francisco. (See the Acknowledgments on page vi for the names of those who made significant contributions to this document.) The document was edited for publishing by Sheila Bruton, working in cooperation with Peter Mangione, Janet Poole, and Mary Smithberger. It was prepared for photo-offset production by the staff of the Bureau of Publications, California Department of Education, under the direction of Theodore R. Smith. The layout and cover were designed by Steve Yee, and typesetting was done by Carey Johnson.

The guide was published by the California Department of Education, 721 Capitol Mall, Sacramento, California (mailing address: P.O. Box 944272, Sacramento, CA 94244-2720). It was distributed under the provisions of the Library Distribution Act and *Government Code* Section 11096.

ISBN 0-8011-0876-4

Ordering Information

Copies of this publication are available for $10 each, plus sales tax for California residents, from the Bureau of Publications, Sales Unit, California Department of Education, P.O. Box 271, Sacramento, CA 95812-0271; FAX 323-0823.

A list of other publications available from the Department appears on page 96. A complete list may be obtained by writing to the address given above or by calling the Sales Unit at (916) 445-1260.

Photo Credits

The California Department of Education gratefully acknowledges the following individuals and organizations for the use of the photos that appear in this publication:

Sheila Signer, cover, pp. 4, 7, 8, 17, 18, 19, 20, 21, 22, 23, 28, 32, 40, 41, 43, 44, 45, 47, 49, 52, 53, 56, 58, 66, 67, 68, 70, 76, 80, 82; Carol Wheeler, pp. 10, 11, 16, 24, 35, 50, 65, 72, 85; Fern Tiger Associates, p. 54.

Contents

Preface

At a time when half the mothers in this country are gainfully employed, most of them full time, more young children require care outside the home than ever before. The growth of child care services has failed to keep pace with the rapidly increasing demand, making appropriate care for young children difficult for families to find. Training is needed to increase the number of quality child care programs, yet the traditional systems for training child care providers are overburdened. In response to this crisis, the California State Department of Education's Child Development Division has developed an innovative and comprehensive approach to training infant and toddler caregivers called The Program for Infant/Toddler Caregivers. The program is a comprehensive training system consisting of a document entitled *Visions for Infant/Toddler Care: Guidelines for Professional Caregiving*, an annotated guide to media training materials for caregivers, a series of training videotapes, and a series of caregiver guides.

The purpose of the caregiver guides is to offer information based on current theory, research, and practice to caregivers in both centers and family child care homes. Each guide addresses an area of infant development and care, covering major issues of concern and related practical considerations. The guides are intended to be used hand in hand with the program's series of videos; the videos illustrate key concepts and caregiving techniques for a specific area of care, and the guides provide extensive and in-depth coverage of a topic.

This guide was written by six noted experts in the field of early social–emotional development and socialization. Like the other guides in the series, this one is rich in practical guidelines and suggestions. The information and ideas presented in this document focus on the caregiver becoming sensitive to the individual traits and needs of infants and toddlers and creating emotionally nurturing relationships with them.

ROBERT W. AGEE
Deputy Superintendent
Field Services Branch

ROBERT A. CERVANTES
Director
Child Development Division

JANET POOLE
Assistant Director
Child Development Division

acknowledgments

This publication was developed by the Center for Child and Family Studies, Far West Laboratory for Educational Research and Development, under the direction of J. Ronald Lally. Special thanks go to Stella Chess, Stanley Greenspan, Jeree Pawl, Alice Honig, and Donna Wittmer, for their contributions of sections to this document; James Johnson, Peter L. Mangione, Sheila Signer, and Kathleen Bertolucci, for editorial assistance; and Virginia Benson, Emily Louw, Janet Poole, Mary Smithberger, and Kathryn Swabel, Child Development Division, California State Department of Education, for review and recommendations on content. Thanks are also extended to the members of the national and California review panels for their comments and suggestions. The national panel members were T. Berry Brazelton, Laura Dittman, Richard Fiene, Magda Gerber, Asa Hilliard, Alice Honig, Jeree Pawl, Sally Provence, Eleanor Szanton, Yolanda Torres, Bernice Weissbourd, and Donna Wittmer. The California panel members were Dorlene Clayton, Dee Cuney, Ronda Garcia, Jacquelyne Jackson, Lee McKay, Janet Nielsen, Pearlene Reese, Maria Ruiz, June Sale, Patty Siegel, and Lenore Thompson.

Introduction

This document contains a wealth of information specifically written to help caregivers with their day-to-day efforts to nurture social and emotional growth in infants and toddlers. This caregiver guide, one of a series developed by The Program for Infant/Toddler Caregivers, is a companion document to *Visions for Infant/Toddler Care: Guidelines for Professional Caregiving.*

The California State Department of Education created *Visions* to describe to the field its understanding of quality care for children under three years of age. *Visions* covers all the major caregiving domains—from providing a safe and healthful learning environment to establishing supportive relationships with families. This guide deals with one of those visions: Vision VII, Development of Each Child's Competence—Social and Emotional Development.

That vision is divided into three areas:

1. The Self: The caregiver provides physical and emotional security for each child and helps each child to know, accept, and take pride in himself or herself and to develop a sense of independence.
2. Social Skills: The caregiver helps each child feel accepted in the group, assists children in learning to communicate and get along with others, and encourages feelings of empathy and mutual respect among children and adults.
3. Guidance: The caregiver provides a supportive environment in which children can begin to learn and practice appropriate and acceptable behaviors as individuals and as a group.

To help caregivers translate these *Vision* statements into specific daily practice, the text that follows presents detailed information about the kind of care young children need for healthy social and emotional development.

The guide is divided into five sections. In the first three sections, nationally recognized experts approach the question of how caregivers can nurture early social and emotional growth. The papers in each section are followed by related information from research and practice, and then concrete examples are given of caregiver actions that support growth.

While each paper focuses on the self, social skills, or guidance, the papers by design overlap. In daily practice, such actions as helping a child develop a positive and realistic sense of self, gain self-esteem, learn the social skills needed to cooperate with others, or follow social rules are not discrete caregiving functions. They all require flexible, individualized care based on responsive trust-building relationships. Each paper, therefore, emphasizes and illustrates an attentive, responsive, and nurturing caregiving approach. Similarly, all the writers stress the critical importance of adapting caregiving techniques to rapidly changing developmental abilities of children as they move from being young infants, to mobile infants, to older toddlers. Thus, for example, J. Ronald Lally's paper shows how the caregiver's role as a provider and adapter shifts as a child moves from infancy to toddlerhood; Jeree H. Pawl's *gifts* become developmentally more sophisticated as children grow older; and Alice S. Honig's and Donna S. Wittmer's paper explains how caregivers must choose different rules and limits to emphasize for each child's stage of development.

Section Four contains appropriate and inappropriate examples of caregiving behavior in the areas of social-emotional growth and socialization. This section draws heavily on the booklet *Developmentally Appropriate Practices,* which is available from the National Association for the Education of Young Children (NAEYC). The information from that booklet is included in Section Four with the permission of NAEYC. Section Five directs the reader to additional readings and appropriate audiovisual materials.

One last important point: Although an attempt was made to make this guide as comprehensive as possible, a decision was made to handle separately two major topics essential to the social-emotional development of infants and toddlers. Those topics are the role of the family and the role of culture. In order to do justice to those important topics, a guide on each of those topics is included in the series of caregiving guides. Those guides are to be used as companion pieces to this document.

the Program for infant toddler caregivers

Section One: The Developing Self

Introduction

In the first paper, Stella Chess, M.D., explains how to recognize important temperamental differences, traits that shape a child's individual style of behavior. She defines and illustrates nine categories of temperament and discusses caregiving approaches best suited to them. Her comments have a direct bearing on the caregiver's role in the development of self and the need for a caregiver's understanding and flexibility in handling children with different temperaments.

Dr. Chess is Professor of Child Psychiatry, New York University Medical Center. She coauthored with Mahin Hassibi the textbook, *Principles and Practice of Child Psychiatry*. For the past 33 years, she and her husband, Alexander Thomas, have directed the New York Longitudinal Study, which established the importance of temperament in child development. In their work, *Behavioral Individuality in Early Childhood, Temperament and Behavior Disorders in Children,* they reported the findings of their longitudinal study. This research significantly altered the study of normal child development and child psychiatry.

In the next paper, Stanley I. Greenspan, M.D., offers a picture of healthy emotional growth during a child's first three years. He charts for caregivers six different stages of emotional development, and he looks at the kinds of early experience necessary to nourish this development. In his paper he demonstrates the importance of providing physically and emotionally secure environments and underscores the role of caregiver as a model for the development of social skills.

Dr. Greenspan is a Clinical Professor of Psychiatry and Behavioral Science and of Child Health and Development at George Washington University Medical School, Washington, D.C., and he is on the academic faculty of Children's Hospital National Medical Center in Washington, D.C. He is the author of *Intelligence and Adaptation*; *Psychopathology and Adaptation in Infancy and Early Childhood*; *The Clinical Interview of the Child: Theory and Practice*; coauthor with Nancy T. Greenspan of *First Feelings: Milestones in the Emotional Development of Your Baby and Child from Birth to Age Four;* and editor of *Infants in Multirisk Families: Case Studies in Preventive Intervention*. Dr. Greenspan is also a practicing child psychiatrist and psychoanalyst.

The Self: Vision Statement

The caregiver provides physical and emotional security for each child and helps each child to know, accept, and take pride in himself or herself and to develop a sense of independence.

All children need a physically and emotionally secure environment that supports their developing self-knowledge, self-control, and self-esteem and at the same time encourages respect for the feelings and rights of others. Flexibility, responsiveness, and emphasis on individualized care for each infant and toddler are especially important in providing this security. Knowing oneself includes knowing about one's body, feelings, and abilities. It also means identifying oneself as a girl or boy and a member of a family and a larger cultural community. Accepting and taking pride in oneself comes from experiencing success and being accepted by others as unique. Self-esteem develops as children master new abilities, experience success as well as failure, and realize their effectiveness in handling increasingly challenging demands in their own ways in an atmosphere of loving attention.

Young infants [birth to nine months], during the first few weeks and months of their lives, begin to build a sense of self-confidence and security in an environment in which they can trust that an adult will lovingly care for their needs. The adult is someone who feeds the child when the child is hungry, keeps the child warm and comfortable, soothes the child when the child is distressed, and provides interesting things to look at, taste, smell, feel, hear, and touch.

For *mobile infants* [six to eighteen months], a loving caregiver provides a home base of warm physical comfort and a safe environment to explore and master. This emotional consistency is essential to developing self-confidence and supporting language, physical, cognitive, and social development.

Toddlers [sixteen to thirty-six months] become aware of many things about themselves, including their separateness from others. A sense of self and growing feelings of independence develop at the same time that toddlers realize the importance of parents and other caregivers. The healthy toddler's inner world is filled with conflicting feelings and ideas: independence and dependence, confidence and doubt, fear and power, hostility and love, anger and tenderness, aggression and passivity. The wide range of toddlers' feelings and actions challenges the resourcefulness and knowledge of the adults who provide emotional security.

This statement is an excerpt from Vision VII, Development of Each Child's Competence—Social and Emotional Development, in *Visions for Infant/Toddler Care: Guidelines for Professional Caregiving* (Sacramento: California State Department of Education, 1988). The *Visions* document outlines the visions or goals of The Program for Infant/Toddler Caregivers.

Temperaments of Infants and Toddlers

Stella Chess, M.D.

Right from the start babies are different. Each has his or her own way of showing feelings and of responding to the world around him or her. These differences, clearly visible in the first few months of life, are expressed in many ways. They can be uncovered by a caregiver who discovers:

- How active the infant is in body movements
- How regular or irregular he or she is in sleeping, feeding, and having bowel movements
- How easily the infant accepts a new food, person, or place
- How long it takes the infant to adjust to a change in his or her schedule or surroundings
- Whether the infant's mood is mainly cheerful, neutral, or fussy
- How sensitive he or she is to loud noises, bright lights, rough clothing, a wet or soiled diaper
- Whether or not the infant can be easily distracted from the activity he or she is engrossed in
- How long the infant persists in giving his or her attention to any single activity

Such traits make up a child's individual style of behaving—his or her *temperament*. Being alert to these temperamental differences and understanding how they require different caregiving approaches are crucial to nurturing children's healthy emotional growth. For example, you may discover:

- That certain children's "headstrong," seemingly cantankerous behavior stems from their temperamental slowness in adapting to new places, people, or games.
- That some toddlers are grumpy a lot and fly off the handle easily because they are unusually sensitive to loud noises and small discomforts.

A better understanding of how temperament works, especially when an infant's or toddler's behavior is exasperating, can help us maintain our own patience and positive attitudes as caregivers. It can also lead us to find the best ways to deal with such behavior. It is important to adjust our responses to fit a particular child's temperament. A caregiving approach that works well with an outgoing, highly expressive child may be less effective, even harmful, with a placid or shy child.

The purpose of this paper is to help you recognize such temperamental differences in very young children so that you can develop ways of relating to

children through their temperament that are best for them. Based on many years of careful research, my husband Alexander Thomas and I found that the behavior of infants and toddlers can be defined according to *nine categories of temperament*, which are identified on the pages that follow.[1]

Before outlining the nine categories of temperament, I need to emphasize a few general points about temperament and its handling:

- Differences in temperament, even at the extremes, are differences in the *normal range of behavior*. All too often a child whose behavior is different from the average is labeled by caregivers and even by mental health professionals as having a behavior problem when, actually, the child is showing only his or her normal temperament. For example, some children are temperamentally inclined to move around a lot. This is a normal trait, not the pathological type of movement called hyperactivity. The key is to try to understand how that particular trait influences the child's behavior and to find the best ways of handling it.

- When caring for a child whose high or low extremes of temperament are troublesome, the goal should not be to insulate and protect the child from those situations which are distressing. That will only restrict the child's life and deny the child valuable opportunities of learning to master social expectations as other children do. Without such experiences children will not develop a basic sense of confidence and self-worth, which come from the proof in actual life that they are capable of coping successfully with the behavioral demands that their world expects of them. Rather, the approach to such a youngster involves finding what we call a "goodness of fit" between caregiver and child. There is a goodness of fit when you handle the child and make demands in a manner that enables the child to meet the demands successfully. When that happens, the child's development can proceed in a healthy direction. If, however, you pressure the child for a quickness and level of adjustment which is beyond the youngster's temperamental ability to achieve, there is a "poorness of fit," with the likelihood that a real behavior problem could develop.

- Do not blame the child if he or she is showing troublesome behavior because of a temperamental trait. The child is not being troublesome deliberately to be malicious or spiteful. Also, do not blame the parents. They may not understand their child's temperament and may, in all good faith, be applying child-rearing rules that do not fit their particular child's temperament.

[1]No one made a full systematic study of these temperamental traits or their influence on the child's psychological development until my husband, Alexander Thomas, and I undertook a project starting in 1956. We started by gathering and analyzing details of the behavior of 133 infants averaging two to three months of age. (We have continued to follow these youngsters and are conducting a new follow-up into their behavior and life-styles, now that they are adults.) In the research project, widely known among professionals as the New York Longitudinal Study, we found that the young infant's behavior could be defined and rated according to nine categories of temperament. Some aspects of temperament can be identified in the newborn, but in general they only begin to be clearly evident by two to three months and very definite by the end of the first year. Some young children show remarkable consistency in temperament from one year to another. Others show less consistency, probably because of the way they are handled by their caregivers and perhaps by differences in rate of brain development, just as normal children vary in the time and way in which they begin to walk or talk. Several research studies have shown a genetic factor in temperament; other biological factors, as yet unknown, are undoubtedly involved in shaping the newborn's temperament. There is no evidence that the parents' handling is the cause of the child's temperament. However, the manner in which the parents or other caregivers respond to the child's temperament may modify, or even change, its expression. Our findings of these nine categories of temperament and their importance for caregiving have been confirmed in recent years in different social classes and cultures by a large number of studies from several research centers in this country as well as from various European and African countries and Japan, India, and Taiwan.

Temperamental Traits and Their Handling

In describing the nine different traits, I will emphasize the extremes in each case—for example, high levels of energy or sensitivity versus low levels—because children with these traits are the ones most likely to need special attention or handling. I will give typical examples of how very young children express such traits and suggest the best caregiving approaches to take.

The majority of children display temperament at a level somewhere in between the extremes of temperament, and these children will fit into home or child care routines fairly easily. In this sense, temperament is similar to intelligence, that is, children of low average or very high intelligence may require special attention, and those of average or slightly superior intelligence will adapt to the routine school curriculum without great difficulty. We will also look at how these specific traits often combine in a child's overall makeup to form certain major patterns of behavior.

1 *Activity Level:* Amount of movement and bodily activity

High Activity

The child who is highly active prefers games and play with a lot of movement; kicks and splashes in the bath, likes to run around. Gets restless and distressed if made to sit quietly in one spot for long periods. Give a child with this level of activity opportunities for active play. If the group is engaged in some quiet activity, let this type of child move around from time to time.

Low Activity

The child with low activity prefers quiet games and can sit calmly looking at picture books or coloring for long periods of time. Because this child moves slowly, he or she is sometimes teased as a slowpoke. You should expect that it will take a child with this level of activity extra time to get things done, such as dressing or moving from one place to another.

2 *Biological Rhythms:* Regularity or irregularity of such functions as sleep-wake cycle, hunger, and bowel elimination

Regularity

The regular child sleeps through the night, takes a regular nap, eats about the same amount from day to day, and has a bowel movement about the same time each day. This child presents no problem with feeding or sleeping schedules and is usually easily toilet trained.

Irregularity

In contrast to the regular child, this one varies in sleep habits and hunger patterns, and he or she may wake up several times at night. The irregular child's big meal may be lunch one day and dinner the next, and his or her bowel movements are unpredictable. You should accept this child's irregular nap and feeding schedules. The child can be trained to sleep through the night if not picked up every time he or she cries. Toilet training will usually take longer and may not succeed until the child learns to be consciously aware of the internal sensation that signals a bowel movement.

3 *Approach/Withdrawal:* How the child responds to a new situation or other stimulus

Approach

The approacher responds positively to a new food by swallowing it, reaches for a new toy, smiles at strangers, and when first joining a play group, plunges right in. Such a child presents few problems to the caregiver, except when this responsiveness is combined with a high level of activity. Then the approacher may run impulsively to climb a new high rock or jungle gym which he or she cannot really manage or try to explore a potentially dangerous object.

Withdraw

Typically cautious about exploring new objects, the withdrawer is likely to push away a new toy or to spit out new food the first few times. Around strangers or when first taken to a new place, this child may fuss or cry and strain to get away. You should be patient with these initial negative reactions. Pressuring the child to make an immediate positive adjustment only increases his or her discomfort and makes it harder for the child to accept new people and things. Instead, small repeated exposures to the unfamiliar let the child gradually overcome his or her early reluctance.

4 *Adaptability:* How quickly or slowly the child adapts to a change in routine or overcomes an initial negative response

High Adaptability

The quickly adaptive child adjusts easily to the family's move to a new home or a visit to a strange place. This child accepts new food that was first rejected after only a few trials, and this child is agreeable to changes in mealtimes and sleeping schedules. Such a child does not usually present problems to a caregiver. Occasionally the youngster may give in too early to unreasonable requests for change, such as a playmate changing the rules in the middle of a game. The quickly adaptive child may benefit by encouragement to "stick to your guns."

Low Adaptability

By contrast, the slowly adaptive child takes a long time to adapt to change or to accept something new he or she originally rejected. Such a child is sometimes misjudged as stubborn or willfully uncooperative. A more accurate term would be cautious. Your approach should be the same as for the withdrawing child—being patient, giving the child a number of exposures to the change, and encouraging the child when he or she begins to show signs of adjusting. Pressure to make such a child adapt very quickly will only boomerang and have the opposite effect.

5 *Quality of Mood:* The amount of pleasant, cheerful, and openly friendly behavior (positive mood) as contrasted with fussing, crying, and openly showing unfriendliness (negative mood)

Positive Mood

Smiling and laughing often, the child whose mood is positive is easily pleased and shows it openly. Fussing and crying are infrequent. This positive mood usually causes positive responses in adults, who find it easy to care for such children.

Negative Mood

The child whose mood is negative tends to fuss or complain a lot, even at trivial discomforts, and cry before going to sleep. This child may show little or no open expression of pleasure, even at games or other events which please, but rather will have a deadpan expression. You should be sure to spot such a child. While not ignoring the child's fussing or complaining, respond cheerfully to him or her. You may find to your surprise that although the child gives no outward evidence of pleasure at some special event, such as an expedition to the zoo, the child later reports it to his or her parents or friends as an exciting, happy event.

6 *Intensity of Reactions:* The energy level of mood expression, whether it is positive or negative

Low Intensity

The low-intensity child expresses both pleasure and discomfort in a low-key way. If happy this child may smile or say quietly that he or she is pleased; if upset the child may whine or say quietly that he or she is unhappy; if upset the child may whine a little or fuss but not loudly. It is easy to misjudge and miss what is going on inside the child if you take the mild reactions as evidence that he or she is not really displeased or upset. Remember that mild expressions may mask strong emotions. Pay careful attention to such expressions and take seriously the feelings behind them.

High Intensity

By contrast, the high-intensity child expresses his or her feelings with great intensity. When happy, this child bubbles and laughs; when upset he or she cries loudly and may even have a tantrum. In this case you have an opposite task: to evaluate objectively whether the issue is important or trivial and not be guided only by the intensive reactions of the child.

7 *Sensitivity Threshold:* How sensitive the child is to potentially irritating stimuli

Low Threshold

The child with a low threshold may be easily upset by loud noises, bright lights, a wet or soiled diaper, or sudden changes in temperature. This child may not be able to tolerate tight socks or clothing with a rough texture. You should be aware of and attend to those reactions but not try to change them.

High Threshold

The child with a high threshold is not bothered by the same kind of stimuli as the child with a low threshold is. You should check regularly to see if the infant has a wet or soiled diaper to avoid diaper rash. Otherwise, this child may be content to suffer the diaper irritation because this child's high threshold keeps him or her from feeling irritated and uncomfortable.

8 *Distractibility:* How easily the child can be distracted from an activity like feeding or playing by some unexpected stimulus—the ringing of a telephone or someone entering the room

High Distractibility

The highly distractible child may start and look up at the sound of a door closing softly. As one parent put it, half the solid food feeding went into the child's ear because she constantly turned her head at small noises or glimpses of movement. In the early childhood period,

Low Distractibility

The child who is not easily distracted tends to stick to an activity despite other noises, conversations, and people around him or her. This is desirable at certain times, such as feeding or dressing, when the child's full attention makes him or her cooperative. But low distractibility

8 Distractibility *(continued)*

High Distractibility

the tendency can be an asset to the caregiver. The child who is fussing at being dressed or is poking at an electric outlet can be easily distracted by showing him or her a toy or other attractive object. In older childhood, however, when persistent concentration on a task like homework is welcomed, high distractibility may not be such a desirable trait.

Low Distractibility

creates a problem if the child is intent on trying to reach a hot stove and will not be easily diverted; the child may have to be removed from the situation.

9 *Persistence/Attention Span:* Two closely related traits, with persistence referring to how long a child will stay with a difficult activity without giving up, and attention span referring to how long the child will concentrate before his or her interest shifts

High Persistence

The highly persistent child with a long attention span will continue to be absorbed in what he or she is doing for long periods of time. In the early childhood years, the highly persistent child is often easy to manage, because once absorbed in an activity, the child does not demand your attention. However, the child may get upset and even have a tantrum if he or she is forced to quit in the middle of an activity, for example, at bedtime, mealtime, or departure time at a child care center. In such cases, you should warn the child in advance if time is limited, or you may decide to prevent the child from starting an activity that will have to be ended abruptly. The highly persistent child may also keep badgering to get something he or she wants, even after a firm refusal.

Low Persistence

The child with low persistence and a short attention span will not stick with a task that is difficult or requires a long period of concentration. If the bead does not go on the string right away, or if the peg does not slip into the hole after a few pokes, the child will give up and move on to something else. This child presents few caregiving problems in the early stages of childhood. Later, however, a short attention span and lack of persistence make learning at school and home difficult.

Three Major Temperamental Patterns

The nine temperamental traits obviously overlap, and they come together in different combinations in a particular child's makeup. We have found that in our country three special combinations of traits are most common: the easy child, the difficult child, and the slow-to-warm-up child.

The Easy Child

Typically, the easy child is regular in biological rhythms, positively approaches most new situations, adapts quickly, and has a predominantly positive mood of low or medium intensity. Such a child is indeed easy for the caregiver. He or she is easily toilet trained, learns to sleep through the night, has regular feeding and nap routines, takes to most new situations and people pleasantly, usually adapts to changes quickly, is generally cheerful, and expresses his or her distress or frustration mildly. In fact, children with "easy" temperaments may show very deep feelings with only a single tear rolling down a cheek. Such children make up about 40 percent of most groups of infants and preschool children.

Occasionally the easy child may have difficulty if he or she has adapted too well to the special standards of the parents, which then come into conflict with the outside world. For example, one child was trained by his parents to be meticulously polite and courteous at all times, with many "thank you," "please," "may I" bows and handshakes, and similar expressions and behavior. However, in his playgroups he stood out as an odd duck and quickly became the butt of their teasing and pranks. The bewildered boy withdrew, completely frustrated. A clinical evaluation of the child and a discussion with the parents quickly clarified the problem. They were able to change their approach, the boy adapted to the new, more acceptable standards of his age-group, and he was welcomed into his peer playgroup.

The Difficult Child

The difficult child is the opposite of the easy child. The child may be hard to train to sleep through the night, his or her

feeding and nap schedules may vary, and the child may be difficult to toilet train because of irregular bowel movements. The difficult child typically fusses or even cries loudly at anything new and usually adapts slowly. All too often this type of child expresses an unpleasant or disagreeable mood and, if frustrated, may even have a temper tantrum. In contrast to the "easy" child's reaction, an intense, noisy reaction by the difficult child may not signify a depth of feeling. Often the best way to handle such outbursts is just to wait them out.

Caregivers who do not understand this type of temperament as normal sometimes feel resentment at the child for being so difficult to manage. They may scold, pressure, or appease the child, which only reinforces his or her difficult temperament and is likely to result in a true behavior problem. Understanding, patience, and consistency, on the other hand, will lead to a "goodness of fit," with a final positive adjustment to life's demands. Then the positive side of the difficult child's high intensity of expression will become evident; the child becomes "lusty" and "full of zest" instead of being labelled "a rotten kid." Only a small minority of children, perhaps 10 percent, fit into the category of the temperamentally difficult child.

The Slow-to-Warm-up Child

Finally, there is the group of children who are usually called shy. The child in this group also has discomfort with the new and adapts slowly, but unlike the difficult child, this child's negative mood is expressed slowly and the child may or may not be irregular in sleep, feeding, and bowel elimination. This is the child who typically stands at the edge of a group and clings quietly to his or her mother when taken to a store, a birthday party, or child care center or school for the first time. If the child is pressured or pushed to join the group, immediately the child's shyness becomes worse. But if allowed to become accustomed to the new surroundings at his or her own pace, to "warm up" slowly, this child can gradually become an active happy member of the group. About 15 percent of the children fit this pattern of the slow-to-warm-up child.

Slow-to-warm-up children may be "invisible" in a group or slip between the cracks. They need attention and special handling to give them extra time to adapt. Then they usually make a wonderful adaptation. The key to working with these children is to go little by little, step by step.

A Combination of Traits

The three types of temperament just outlined are very useful in providing effective care for children, but they do not tell the whole story. If you add the percents quoted for the three patterns— 40 for the easy child, 10 for the difficult child, and 15 for the slow-to-warm-up child—the percents do not add up to 100. That is because some children's mixtures of temperament do not fit easily into one of those patterns. Furthermore, different children who can be called *easy, difficult,* or *slow-to-warm-up* temperamentally may vary in the way they express the individual traits which make up their overall pattern. One difficult child may be very irregular but only moderately intense, while another may be just the opposite, and so on.

Although we speak of difficult temperament in terms of the combination of traits outlined earlier, some children's care may be difficult for other temperamental reasons. A child with a low sensory threshold may be irritated by tight clothing, while other children with a higher sensory threshold will not be bothered. The child may fuss and struggle while he or she is being dressed and try to pull the clothes off. If you do not understand that the problem is sensitive skin, the child will be difficult to manage. In this and many other cases, there can be a difficult child whose temperament is not appreciated. Nevertheless, it is useful to keep in mind the notion of difficult temperament in terms of the combination of traits described earlier because children who exhibit a difficult temperament are most likely to require your special understanding and handling.

A Final Word

If the caregiver observes the child's behavior in a number of situations on a number of days without making value judgments that label the child as nice, stubborn, aggressive, uncooperative, and so forth, it is usually relatively easy for the caregiver to identify a child's temperament, especially at the extremes. If the caregiver then adopts the approach which helps the child function in a healthy, desirable way, and succeeds with time, the change confirms the caregiver's evaluation. We have found that many caregivers are able, even intuitively, to spot a child's temperament that is causing a problem of management and figure out how to deal with the issue, even though they have never heard of the concept of temperament. There are, of course, some cases in which a child's problem behavior may be caused or complicated by some psychiatric disorder. In such instances the caregiver's efforts may not be effective, and a mental health professional's evaluation may be necessary.

A child's temperament and the caregiver's response to it can be a highly important factor in the child's emotional development. The child's behavior with peers, relatives, and adults and the feedback he or she gets from them, as well as the variety of life experiences to which the child is exposed, all contribute to the self-image the child develops.

If the child has discomfort with new situations, patient encouragement will overcome that initial shyness, and the child will gain increasing confidence in his or ability to make friends and to master new challenges. If children who have intense negative reactions when frustrated learn that they get what they want if they have loud and long tantrums, their emotional development may result in their becoming "nasty brats." The highly active girl whose motor energy is channeled into useful directions will be pleased and happy with the approval this gains for her. If, however, she is left to her own devices, her physical energies may make her restless and even disruptive in group games, and she may be labeled a spoilsport and be scapegoated by her peers.

Thus any temperamental attribute may become either an asset or a liability to a child's development, depending on whether the caregivers recognize what type of approach is best suited for that child. The aim is not to indulge a child to become self-centered and fixed in his or her behavioral tendencies. Quite the contrary. Having an appreciation of children's individual temperaments makes it possible to use the knowledge to help children mature into socially adaptable and welcome members of the society in which they will grow up.

Chart One: The Temperament Assessment Scale

By answering the following questions for each child, you can increase your understanding of the temperaments of the children you serve. Refer to Dr. Chess's paper to help complete the scale.

1. *Activity Level.* How much does the child wiggle and move around when being read to, sitting at a table, or playing alone?

    Active   1   3   5   Quiet

2. *Regularity.* Is the child regular about eating times, sleeping times, amount of sleep needed, and bowel movements?

    Regular   1   3   5   Irregular

3. *Adaptability.* How quickly does the child adapt to changes in his or her schedule or routine? How quickly does the child adapt to new foods and places?

    Adapts quickly   1   3   5   Slow to adapt

4. *Approach/Withdrawal.* How does the child usually react the first time to new people, new foods, new toys, and new activities?

    Initial approach   1   3   5   Initial withdrawal

5. *Physical Sensitivity.* How aware is the child of slight noises, slight differences in temperature, differences in taste, and differences in clothing?

    Not sensitive   1   3   5   Very sensitive

6. *Intensity of Reaction.* How strong or violent are the child's reactions? Does the child laugh and cry energetically, or does he or she just smile and fuss mildly?

    High intensity   1   3   5   Mild reaction

7. *Distractibility.* Is the child easily distracted or does he or she ignore distractions? Will the child continue to work or play when other noises or children are present?

    Very distractible   1   3   5   Not distractible

8. *Positive or Negative Mood.* How much of the time does the child show pleasant, joyful behavior compared with unpleasant crying and fussing behavior?

    Positive mood   1   3   5   Negative mood

9. *Persistence.* How long does the child continue with one activity? Does the child usually continue if it is difficult?

    Long attention span   1   3   5   Short attention span

Emotional Development in Infants and Toddlers

Stanley I. Greenspan, M.D.

Today, just as in past decades, some children grow into depressed adults and some feel fulfilled; some act impulsively, flaunt social rules, or take drugs, and others are responsible, respectful, and law abiding. But today, in contrast to earlier years, we know enough about how to treat children when they are very young that we can help prevent later difficulties and foster healthy personalities. Being aware of this emerging body of information, therefore, is of crucial importance to parents and caregivers of very young children.

In my book, *First Feelings: Milestones in the Emotional Development of Your Baby and Child from Birth to Age Four,* I described in detail a picture of the healthy emotional development of children from birth to age four and the types of early experiences I believe are necessary to nourish this growth. As caregivers know, it becomes their task to provide those experiences when the parent is absent, but knowing how to do that can be very confusing. The $64,000 question is: "What can caregivers do to help infants and toddlers develop healthy emotional behavior?" I believe the answer must always begin with a solid understanding of the stages of children's emotional development:

Stages of Emotional Development

There are six basic stages in a child's healthy emotional development from birth to about four years of age:

Stage One: Self-regulation and Interest in the World (Age: 0 months +)
Stage Two: Falling in Love (Age: 4 months +)
Stage Three: Purposeful Communication (Age: 8 months +)
Stage Four: Beginning of a Complex Sense of Self (Age: 10 months +)
Stage Five: Emotional Ideas (Age: 18 months +)
Stage Six: Emotional Thinking (Age: 30 months +)

Stage One: Self-regulation and Interest in the World

During the first stage, which is from birth to about four months, the babies are learning to take an interest in sights, sounds, touch, smell, and movement. Babies are also learning to calm themselves down. We find that even during the first weeks of life, as the earlier paper on temperament emphasizes, children respond to care differently. For example, some babies are especially sensitive:

- Babies overly sensitive to touch will pull away and arch their backs. These same babies love a firm, gentle squeeze. Firm pressure helps them relax.
- Some babies are sensitive to high-pitched noises. In response to baby talk, they will startle. These babies do very well with low-pitched sounds.
- Some babies love to be moved quickly or whirled around in space. For others too quick a movement is scary.

Babies are different, too, in their ability to soothe themselves or let themselves be soothed. For example:

- Some babies can, from day one, take their fist, put it in their mouths, and calm themselves down. Other babies cannot find their mouths.
- Some babies cuddle and nuzzle easily; others feel either too stiff or too loose. They cannot seem to get their muscles at the right tone.

In addition, babies differ in their abilities to understand the messages their senses take in. The ability to make sense of a caregiver's sounds, learned during the first two to three months of life, varies from baby to baby. Some babies can take in lots of baby talk and eagerly look at their caregiver for more. Others become confused by complex rhythms of baby talk and by fast talk, but if the caregiver goes slower and makes only a few distinct sounds, the baby will understand and watch the caregiver's face for more messages.

It is very important for caregivers to detect these individual differences in order to understand the basis for each baby's developing interest in the world. Learn what is special about each infant's way of dealing with sensations, taking in and acting on information, and finding ways to organize his or her movements to

calm or soothe himself or herself; then act accordingly. What a caregiver does early is important.

Stage Two: Falling in Love

By four months of age, babies are in the second stage of emotional development, a stage in which they need to be wooed into loving relationships. Babies also differ in the ways they act during this stage. There are the more passive "laid back" babies who need to be sold on the human world, and there are those who eagerly reach out and embrace their caregivers.

Caregivers who are not afraid to feel rejected and who do not take a particular baby's lack of interest as a personal insult can do the baby a world of good. Such caregivers can try many different "wooing" tactics based on a sensitive reading of what the baby shows he or she likes and does not like. Facial expressions, holding positions, types of touch and pressure, and sounds can all be used to communicate the experience of falling in love.

Stage Three: Purposeful Communication

By eight months of age, babies need experiences which verify that their signals are being read. Dependency (reaching out), assertiveness, curiosity, and even aggression are now part of a give-and-take, cause-and-effect pattern in which caregiver and baby "read" and respond to each other. Sometimes the amount of exploration and excitement generated by new and different experiences during this period can lead to the caregiver overstimulating the infant, as in this example:

The new caregiver holds the infant's hands and wrestles his head into the infant's stomach. The infant pulls away. Instead of changing his action, the caregiver does it again, trying to get the infant to give a pleasurable response. The infant pulls away again, but the caregiver keeps trying to get something going, almost as if he were playing with a dog or cat.

Experienced caregivers know better than to do what the new caregiver did in the above example. The experienced caregivers are usually involved in constant "signal reading." They know when to do more with the infant and when to do less. Neither overstimulating nor understimulating the child, caregivers model how purposeful communication should go. By respecting the infant's messages, caregivers model respect of others for the infant.

Stage Four: Beginning of a Complex Sense of Self

By ten to eighteen months of age, babies need to be admired for all the new abilities they have mastered. They have organized their abilities into schemes to get things done and make things happen. The babies are inventive and show initiative, as in Suzy's case:

> Suzy takes her caregiver's hand, walks to the refrigerator, bangs on the door, and once the door has been opened, points to the food she wants.

By acknowledging the child who completes such a complex action as Suzy's, the caregiver contributes to that child's developing sense of self. When caregivers engage in complex play with the child and intellectually expand the play, they model new ways for the child to grow. For example:

> Johnny chases you; you scoot around and double back on him. Johnny giggles with glee and the next time scoots around and doubles back on you. Johnny has increased the complexity of his behavior plan and his behavior.

Lots of imitation happens at this point in children's development, and so does the beginning of pretend play. By allowing for and taking part in early games and imitation play, caregivers help children expand their sense of themselves as complex organized persons—of *me* and *not me*.

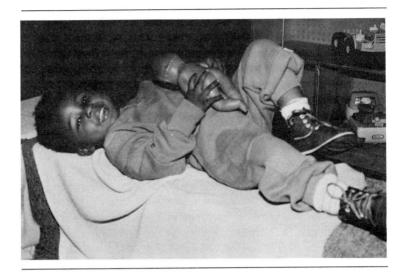

Stage Five: Emotional Ideas

By eighteen to twenty-four months of age, children are able to create images in their minds. Their pretending to be someone else is a sign of that, as illustrated in this example:

> By cuddling his doll and calling it his baby brother, the toddler engages in fantasy. The two-year-old is able to create images in his mind's eye as if he were watching a movie of mommy and daddy, his baby brother, and himself.

During this fifth stage in the emotional development of children, caregivers can be of great help if they help children express their feelings as emotional ideas rather than just act them out. Make-believe play is wonderful for such expression because children begin to use words and gestures to label their feelings. Caregivers can provide young children a safe way to put into words their curiosity about sexuality, aggression, rejection, and separation through make-believe play. The expression of emotional ideas is very releasing to a child but sometimes uncomfortable for adults. If caregivers find that they are having trouble letting children put those feelings into words, turning to other caregivers may help. As a caregiver, you may be quite comfortable allowing children to explore competition and anger but find that you cut off imaginative play about closeness and separation. By getting help with "hot spots" and "blind spots," you will open up more emotional areas to the child for his or her exploration.

Stage Six: Emotional Thinking

When children are about 30 months old, their emotional development involves shifting gears between make-believe and reality. In this sixth stage of their development, young children are beginning to have the ability to reason about their feelings instead of only being able to act them out in pretend play.

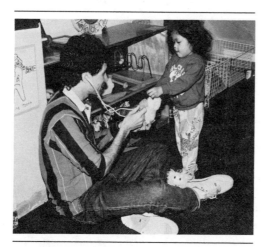

During this stage of emotional thinking, setting limits and discipline become very important. However, limit setting must always be balanced with empathy and an interest in what the child is feeling. Here, too, caregivers need to look at themselves. Some caregivers who are very indulgent do well with the pretend-play side but are very weak on the limit-setting side; some who are law and order people do well on the limit-setting side

but are very weak on the make-believe play and empathy side.

A general rule is that as caregivers increase limit setting, particularly with an impulsive child, they must increase the empathy and concern for the child's feelings and make-believe. The best way to encourage empathy is with what I call "floor time." This is one-to-one play where the caregiver follows the child's lead and encourages make-believe and friendly chit-chat.

Emotional Strengths and Their Development

Once caregivers understand the six basic stages of emotional development, they have a clearer understanding of what

---

Healthy Emotional Development of the Child at Age Three or Four

1. Has warm, trusting, intimate relationships with other children and adults
2. Shows positive self-esteem: feels good about what he or she does
3. Uses good control of impulses and behavior; handles assertiveness, curiosity, and angry protests in ways that are in accord with:
   a. Society's goals
   b. Norms for peer group
   c. The settings the child finds himself or herself in, such as preschool, church, playground
4. Separates make-believe from reality and adjusts to the demands of reality
5. Exhibits a rich imagination:
   a. Incorporates and labels feelings
   b. Uses words to express needs, feelings, and ideas
6. Shows empathy and compassion for others; deals with loss and the limitations of life
7. Concentrates, focuses, and plans as a basis for learning in educational settings

they can do to help children in that development. I have found that visualizing how emotionally healthy three- and four-year-old children function helps me decide best how infants and toddlers should be treated so that they will develop healthy emotional behavior. In order to clarify your role in children's emotional development, I suggest that you review the accompanying list of qualities of healthy emotional development as part of your planning of day-to-day activities with infants and toddlers. Conduct your review with this question in mind: "Are my daily actions helping the young children I serve move toward emotional health now and at age three or four?"

After caregivers have a clear view of what constitutes healthy emotional development, they need to explore how children develop emotional strengths throughout the six stages of emotional development or how they develop negative traits instead.

Capacity for Intimacy

During the first few months of life, babies are beginning to take an interest in the world:

- The newborn pays attention to sights and sounds.
- By two to four months, the infant shows a preference for the human world.
- By eight months, that intimacy takes a more active form.
- By sixteen months of age, a child's capacity for intimacy reaches a new level. The child can carry a feeling of intimacy in his or her mind.

Based on memory of past events and through vision and hearing, children can understand gestures and even some words, and they can feel love from clear across the room. Children do not have to go to the caregiver and physically make contact, but they learn to feel close.

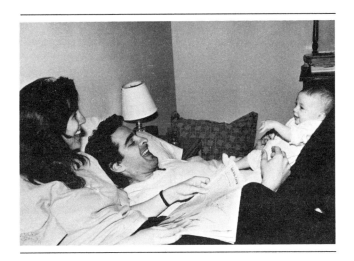

As children get a little older, they continue to develop the capacity for intimacy:

- By eighteen months to three years of age, the child has the ability to create images and emotional ideas in his or her own mind.
- Dolls can be made to put each other to sleep or to feed, to spank, or to hug one another.
- When the caregiver is temporarily in the other room and the parent is gone, the child can hold mental images of the loved one and not feel abandoned, even while the child waits for that loved one to return.

- Between two and one-half and four years of age, the child learns how his or her feelings influence someone else.
- The child's intellect is developed enough to hold the idea that "being nice leads someone else to be nice."

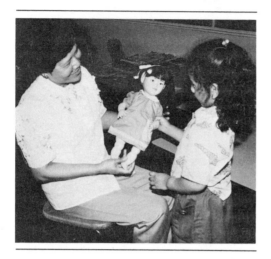

When children's emotional development progresses as described, all is well. But sometimes caregivers will find that they have infants in their care who are not developing intimacy in normal ways. Some of the progressive signs that young children are having trouble developing intimate relationships are these:

- By two to four months, the child is looking despondent or sad. When the parent or caregiver comes into the room, the child may look indifferent and stare off into space.
- By eight months instead of reaching out and gesturing "Give me a hug; I want closeness," the baby turns away, arches his or her back when approached, and prefers play objects to human contact. This child vocalizes, reaches, and moves but not in relation to the caregiver; rather the child responds in a passive, chaotic, or disorganized way, seemingly without purpose.
- By fifteen months the child may not only avoid human contact but also bite

or kick when someone tries to make contact.
- By eighteen months the child may consistently refuse to be picked up and shake his or her head "no" or say no.
- By two or three years of age, the child is often either provocative and negative or passive, without spark, and does what he or she is told but without interest. *People are treated as things—no different from a toy.*

When caregivers see the preceding behaviors, they need to pay special attention to the emotional needs of the infants and intervene through their own efforts or by seeking outside help.

Self-esteem

A caregiver can observe self-esteem blooming in the emotionally healthy four-month-old child who greets the world optimistically and the eight-month-old who vigorously explores the caregiver's nose, mouth, and hair.

During the later part of the first and most of the second year of life, infants'

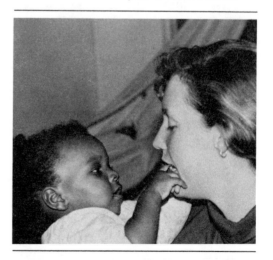

self-esteem can be seen quite markedly in their vigorous exploration of the outer limits of the family child care home or center. When caregivers enthusiastically join in the exciting searching games, the shared experience and mutual admiration show the child that his or her growing inclination to explore is something to feel good about.

It is important that toddlers admire themselves and feel proud of their actions. Those feelings develop when children have caregivers who can figure out what is special about each child and share their enjoyment of that specialness with him or her.

The three-year-old does not always need the caregiver to praise him or her for completing a puzzle. The child can imagine the caregiver saying, "Gee, that's a terrific job you did with the puzzle." The pride the caregiver has so often shown becomes part of the child.

Limit-setting by caregivers is also a critical part of building self-esteem. Children who are not secure that they will be helped to control their anger are often too frightened to feel good about themselves.

In helping children develop high self-esteem, caregivers need to understand what causes children to have low self-esteem, as outlined here:

- By four months of age, some children are already relating to people in a cautious way. These children show more than just temperamental caution. They act as though they expect to be rejected. Joe reaches out to the caregiver a little bit, looks, then turns away with movements and expressions that say, "I expect to be rejected."
- At eight months, when he returns to care after a weekend and sees the caregiver, Harold looks away as if to say, "You're going to have to woo me back. Show you love me." If the caregiver is too sensitive to this rejection or too busy ("I don't have the time to bend over backwards for you"), Harold's fear that he is not loved might deepen. It is common for some infants to look away from a loved one after a separation, but the infant with low self-esteem makes "looking away" a pattern of relating.

- The fifteen-month-old child who looks sad or fearful and hardly ever insists, "Do it my way!" shows low self-esteem.

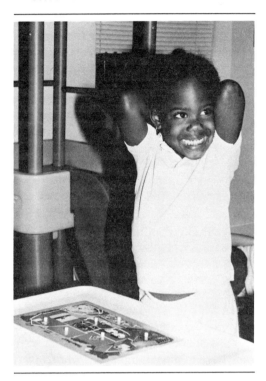

- Eighteen-month-old children who are so fragile that it is impossible for them to do things any other way but their own will do things differently only if threatened.
- By two and one-half years, some children expect to fail at everything they do. Sara knocks down the blocks before the tower is built. Paul messes up the puzzle before the puzzle is completed.

Impulse Control

As early as eight months of age, crawling babies will respond when a caregiver says, "Don't touch that!" They may look up and then go back to trying to touch it, but they listen. That is the beginning of behavior and impulse control. By the fifth time they hear, "Don't touch it," they may stop.

Even at eight or nine months of age, babies are beginning to learn about limits and controls. The caregiver helps by using gentle, consistent, and considerate words and gestures to let the child know what is allowed and what is not. By the second year of life, the toddler has learned to value and use that outside help to establish his or her own limits. By the time children are eighteen months old, they are quite capable of listening and attending to what a caregiver wishes them to do and not do.

When Johnny wants to do something "bad," such as mark on the wall, the caregiver should let him know that it is not allowed: "You can't mark on the wall. Here is some paper to mark on." Johnny may see this as a game, but through the game he will learn to understand the caregiver's wishes and some of the rules people live by. Specific guidance techniques can be found in the paper by Alice Honig and Donna Wittmer, which appears later in this guide.

Words, gestures, eye-to-eye messages, backed up by caregiver action when necessary, provide the eighteen-month-old child an opportunity to learn about limits. *But always balance the limits with time for spontaneous play.*

By three years of age, children will be using internal images to develop and understand rules. Caregivers can see this happen in children's more complex games and fantasy play.

Caregivers also need to be aware of the signs indicating that children are having trouble controlling their impulses:

- Healthy children will break rules, and they will challenge you. But they are continually learning, and caregivers can see their progress. Children who have not progressed may not be able to control their impulses because they do not have the foundations. They may have never learned at eight to fourteen months how to respond to limiting gestures and words. If they have received few limiting guidelines, there has been no opportunity to learn, for example, if they did something inappropriate and were simply ignored or pulled away with no clarifying words or gestures.
- Humans respond to cues that help them to know what is okay and not okay. If children have had much of their behavior limited (too much control), those children will break rules and overstep limits defiantly or sneakily because those are the only ways the children have found to express themselves.

Distinction Between Reality and Fantasy

How do children learn to distinguish what is real from what is pretend? The process begins with falling in love. To the four-month-old infant, the human relationship—with the parent and with the caregiver—is the carrier not only of warmth and security but also of reality. The child might wonder: "Where do I end, and where does the caregiver begin?" "Who is doing the soothing?" The answers to those questions are very vague to the four-month-old baby. By eight months of age, the child has had a little more experience and is starting to learn about cause and effect: "I cry. She comes." "I smile. She smiles back." The baby's dependency is real and so is the closeness of the relationship. For example:

- When a baby reaches out to be picked up, a human being has to be there who will read the signal accurately and respond by picking the child up.
- When a baby is interested in exploring and being curious, he or she needs a human being who will respond to that curiosity by saying, "Gee, you're doing great!"
- When a baby is being aggressive, looking the caregiver in the eye and pushing food off the plate as if to say, "What are you going to do about it?" the baby needs to hear how the caregiver really feels.

The eight-month-old child needs to learn that what he or she does will affect people differently. The child's anger, protests, and smiles all receive different responses. The child is also defining the "realness" of who he or she is. If the child who is reaching out to be picked up receives a message that says, "Stop it, you're exhausting me, leave me alone," that child will come to define himself or herself as too demanding. Those types of messages from caregivers can lead to confusion in a child: "Gee, I thought I just wanted a hug."

By ten months of age, dependency and closeness, assertiveness and curiosity, and aggression and protest are being defined. The child not only learns from the feedback that comes from caregivers of the reality of *me* acting on *you* but also begins to define what kind of me is acting on what kind of you. Reality testing, human to human, child to caregiver, is the way that children learn what is real and what they think is real about themselves.

The early reality testing ("If I reach out I will be picked up.") and its healthy development through the six basic stages of a child's emotional development leads to a child who, at age two, has a sense of what he or she thinks and how those

thoughts relate to the real world. The child who has not participated in the reality-checking experience (with a sensitive caregiver who understands the need for accurate feedback) becomes either a child with a distorted sense of who he or she is and what to expect from adults or a child unable to distinguish very well between fantasy and reality.

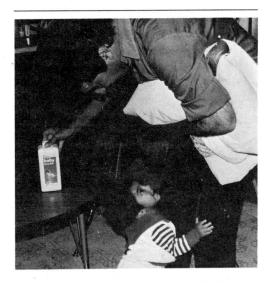

An important job for the caregiver of the two- to three-year-old child is the ability to balance limit-setting, reality, and make-believe. A caregiver who can play the role of the baby in the dress-up area, announce that it is time to eat lunch, set forth the rules, "You can't bite," and

switch back and forth in the roles with
• little effort makes similar switches from
reality to fantasy and back again easy for
the child to make.

Imagination, Creativity, and Curiosity

The explorative touch of the four-
month-old baby, the crawl to the distant
ball by the infant at eight months of age,
the climb to reach the toy on the top shelf
by the twenty-month-old toddler, and the
make-believe play of the three-year-old
child are all part of the early work of
imagination, creativity, and curiosity. But
just what should be encouraged and why?
For example:

A two and one-half-year-old takes a
stick and pretends it is a gun or takes a
plastic gun and says "bang, bang." Is
that good or bad?

Make-believe must be encouraged.
Starting at about two years of age and
sometimes earlier, make-believe play is a
way for children to release and understand their deepest emotions. When
make-believe play is allowed or encouraged, the child learns how to change the

actions of hitting, biting, kicking, scream-
ing, and crying to ideas he or she can
explore. In other words, pretend play
should be thought of as the gymnasium
for exercising emotional ideas.

For example, a child learns, through
having dolls fight, to experiment with
aggression in a safe way. Pretend play
also:

• Helps the child get to the stage where
  he or she can say, "This is okay to do
  in make-believe, but it's not okay to
  do for real. It could hurt someone."
• Gives the child a chance to learn to
  identify feelings.
• Teaches the child to reason about
  anger.

The eighteen-month-old to four-year-
old child must learn to take his or her
feelings and move them into the world of
ideas. By using words to express feelings
in make-believe play, that movement is
accomplished. Those make-believe
dramas about separation, rejection, punishment, hugging, and feeding are the
building blocks for emotional thinking,
the ability to reason about feelings. Look
what reasoning about feelings does for
adults. The emotionally healthy adult can
say, "I'm angry," and reasoning about the
anger, he or she can look for other
options. One option may be: "I have no
reason to be angry. I'm just self-centered.
That's why I get angry all the time." Or
another option: "I have a good reason to
be angry this time. I shouldn't be treated
like this and I'm going to take steps to
change things."

If parents and caregivers do not allow
for practice of emotional reasoning,
children will get stuck at an infantile
level of emotional expression. The older
child may act out feelings as a much
younger child might and get shamed or in
trouble for those actions. An older child
may also stifle feelings as a younger
child might by restricting *any* release of
feelings, including appropriate use of
words.

At about the age of three years, a child will begin to say, "I feel sad. I didn't get what I wanted." Those feelings are expressed in play with dolls, too. Three-year-old children become more and more conscious about winning and losing. They express madness or sadness. Caregivers can help by giving children a chance to express how they feel about loss and losing and to "get into the skin" of others who may be feeling the same things, as in the following example:

> "Oh, it's great for he-man Billy, he beat the other guy up, but how does the other guy feel?"

> "Well, I think he is sad, Mrs. Coffey."

> "Do you ever feel sad?"

> "I feel sad when I don't get a toy, or when I miss my mommy or daddy."

Sadness is a natural and valid human emotion. It is an important emotion in learning to accept limits. Sadness is also the basis for empathy and compassion. A person cannot empathize with other people's sadness, loss, or hurt unless that person can experience those feelings himself or herself. Children can use the caregiver's help to "walk in other people's shoes." Giving young children the opportunity to see how their actions feel to the other person is a critical caregiving assignment. Not giving children the chance to empathize, or modeling selfish behavior for them to imitate, deprives children of one of the most mature emotions known to human-kind.

The Caregiver's Role

In this paper we have seen that children need the caregiver's help as children move through the various stages of emotional development. Children need to create intimate relationships, develop a positive self-esteem, attain impulse control, define their sense of reality, expand their capacity for imagination, gain an ability to deal with loss, and learn to empathize with the feelings of others. In the past, much of the assistance in children's emotional development was provided in a hit-or-miss way. That assistance usually was not part of a caregiver's training, but many caregivers knew how important the help was and intuitively and naturally provided it. My studies of the stages of emotional development and the needs of children growing through those stages are intended to help caregivers who would like to pay closer attention to children's emotional development.

Chart Two: Baby's Emotional Milestones

I. Self-regulation and Interest in the World—Birth to 3 months

Increasingly (but still only sometimes):
—Able to calm down
—Sleeps regularly
—Brightens to sights (by alerting and focusing on object)
—Brightens to sounds (by alerting and focusing on your voice)
—Enjoys touch
—Enjoys movement in space (up and down, side to side)

II. Falling in Love—2 to 7 months

When wooed, increasingly (but still only sometimes):
—Looks at you with a special, joyful smile
—Gazes at you with great interest
—Joyfully smiles at you in response to your vocalizations
—Joyfully smiles at you in response to your interesting facial expressions
—Vocalizes back as you vocalize

III. Developing Intentional Communication—3 to 10 months

Increasingly (but still only sometimes) responds to:
—Your gestures with gestures in return (you hand her a rattle and she takes it)
—Your vocalizations with vocalizations
—Your emotional expressions with an emotional response (a smile begets a smile)
—Pleasure or joy with pleasure
—Encouragement to explore with curiosity (reaches for interesting toy)

Increasingly (but still only sometimes) initiates:
—Interactions (expectantly looks for you to respond)
—Joy and pleasure (woos you spontaneously)
—Comforting (reaches up to be held)
—Exploration and assertiveness (explores your face or examines a new toy)

IV. The Emergence of an Organized Sense of Self—9 to 18 months

Increasingly (but still only sometimes):
—Initiates a complex behavior pattern such as going to refrigerator and pointing to
  desired food, playing a chase game, rolling a ball back and forth with you
—Uses complex behavior in order to establish closeness (pulls on your leg and
  reaches up to be picked up)

This chart is reprinted from Stanley Greenspan's and Nancy T. Greenspan's *First Feelings: Milestones in the Emotional Development of Your Baby and Child from Birth to Age Four* (New York: Viking Penguin, Inc., 1985). Copyright © Stanley Greenspan, M.D., and Nancy Thorndike Greenspan, 1985. Used with permission.

—Uses complex behavior to explore and be assertive (reaches for toys, finds you in another room)
—Plays in a focused, organized manner on own
—Examines toys or other objects to see how they work
—Responds to limits that you set with your voice or gestures
—Recovers from anger after a few minutes
—Able to use objects like a comb or telephone in semirealistic manner
—Seems to know how to get you to react (which actions make you laugh, which make you mad)

V. Creating Emotional Ideas—18 to 36 months

Increasingly (but still only sometimes):
—Engages in pretend play with others (puts doll to sleep, feeds doll, has cars or trucks race)
—Engages in pretend play alone
—Makes spatial designs with blocks or other materials (builds a tower, lines up blocks)
—Uses words or complex social gestures (pointing, sounds, gestures) to express needs or feelings ("me, mad" or "no, bed")
—Uses words or gestures to communicate desire for closeness (saying "hug" or gesturing to sit on your lap)
—Uses words or gestures to explore, be assertive and/or curious ("come here" and then explores toy with you)
—Able to recover from anger or temper tantrum and be cooperative and organized (after 5 or 10 minutes)

Later in stage and throughout next, increasingly (but still only sometimes):
—Uses your help and some toys to play out pretend drama dealing with closeness, nurturing, or care (taking care of favorite stuffed animal)
—Uses your help and some toys to play out pretend drama dealing with assertiveness, curiosity, and exploration (monsters chasing, cars racing, examining dolls' bodies)
—Pretend play becomes more complex, so that one pretend sequence leads to another (instead of repetition, where the doll goes to bed, gets up, goes to bed, etc., the doll goes to bed, gets up, and then gets dressed, or the cars race, crash, and then go to get fixed)
—Spatial designs become more complex and have interrelated parts, so that a block house has rooms or maybe furniture, a drawing of a face has some of its parts

VI. Emotional Thinking: The Basis for Fantasy, Reality, and Self-esteem—30 to 48 months

Increasingly (but still only sometimes):
—Knows what is real and what isn't
—Follows rules
—Remains calm and focused
—Feels optimistic and confident
—Realizes how behavior, thoughts, and feelings can be related to consequences (if behaves nicely, makes you pleased; if naughty, gets punished; if tries hard, learns to do something)
—Realizes relationship between feelings, behavior, and consequences in terms of being close to another person (knows what to do or say to get a hug, or a back rub)

—Realizes relationship between feelings, behavior, and consequences in terms of assertiveness, curiosity, and exploration (knows how to exert will power through verbal, emotional communication to get what he wants)
—Realizes relationship between feelings, behavior, and consequences in terms of anger (much of time can respond to limits)
—Interacts in socially appropriate way with adults
—Interacts in socially appropriate way with peers

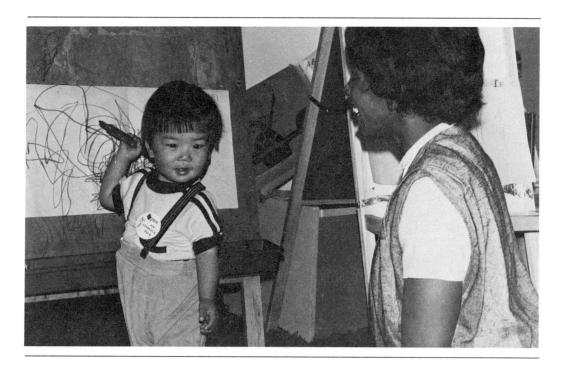

Chart Three: The Caregiver's Role in the Child's Development of Self

How to Help Develop the Capacity for Intimacy:

—Be warm and interesting.
—Be patient, position yourself so the baby can see you and is secure.
—Anticipate a baby's attention span for intimacy; before fussiness begins, switch to another activity, then later return to wooing.
—For a withdrawn baby, look for and respond to the baby's fleeting gestures.
—For a hyperexcitable baby, soothe and woo the baby with calming gestures.
—Woo the baby, let the infant learn about love from you.
—Set aside time for pleasant and loving exchanges.
—Tolerate and continue to woo a baby who is upset or protesting.
—Fine-tune your wooing efforts.
—For an excitable or fretful baby, become calm and subtle.

How to Help Develop Self-esteem:

—Admire the child's new abilities.
—Be a good follower.
—Determine a behavior that is easy for the baby to do; use the behavior for interacting.
—For a baby who is a low sender, react to any signal the baby sends.
—For an excitable baby, relax the baby and make the interaction relaxing and enjoyable.
—Bring the baby back to organized behavior when the baby is being disorganized.
—Help the child expand the complexity of his or her play.
—Recognize the child's need for balance between independence and security.
—Stay emotionally involved and available while you are setting limits.

How to Help Develop Impulse Control:

—Pay attention to which patterns help a baby recover after stress.
—Use those patterns, then stop to see if the baby tries to continue on his or her own to woo you and calm down.
—Help a child practice relating cause-and-effect interactions through language and respond logically to the child's communication; do not ignore communication or change the subject.
—Do not let a child's aggression frighten you.
—Go "eyeball-to-eyeball" with a child when he or she is angry; help the child regain control; set firm limits.
—Reengage a child after an explosion.

This chart is adapted from Stanley Greenspan's and Nancy T. Greenspan's *First Feelings: Milestones in the Emotional Development of Your Baby and Child from Birth to Age Four* (New York: Viking Penguin, Inc., 1985). Used with permission.

How to Help Children Learn the Differences Between Fantasy and Reality:

—Gently introduce into a child's play an emotion the child avoids.
—Add on logical sequences when a child's difficulty with an emotion causes him or her to make an abrupt shift in the story.
—Pay attention to how you handle any emotion a child seems to be uncomfortable with.
—When the intensity of an emotion causes a child to become excitable or withdrawn, be alert to when the intensity is too much; provide more structure at that time to reengage the child; encourage the child to talk about his or her feelings; help the child put actions into words.
—Encourage a child to integrate opposite, emotional feelings toward one person.
—With the child who overindulges in fantasy, ensure you are providing enough security and setting effective limits; give the context for when the fantasy is appropriate.
—With the child who overindulges the reality orientation, look for family stress and lack of emotional support; gradually introduce the idea of fantasy into conversation and play.
—Make sure a child understands the functional role of objects, people, and feelings.

How to Help Develop Imagination, Creativity, and Curiosity:

—Allow a child to dictate how playtime is spent.
—Follow a child's lead in conversation or play.
—Respect individuality.
—Encourage the use of senses and movement in new ways.
—Begin with the activity a baby does best.
—Gradually add on activities that encourage the baby to use other senses and motor systems.
—Through pretend play, help the child go one step further in his or her story either by adding more characters to the scene or by shifting the concept of the characters.

How to Help Develop Empathy:

—Become a partner and provide both physical and emotional warmth during your playtimes; invite other children to play.
—If a child is not involved in emotional, cause-and-effect exchanges, use the child's involvement in pretend play to woo him or her into those exchanges.
—Become the child's partner and gently introduce emotional themes into the play.
—Establish contact after a disruption. ("I'm sorry I shouted at you. I want to give you a hug.")
—Help a child to reengage emotional ideas. ("You know I get mad at you when you dump your toy basket. Why do you want to do it?")
—Respect a child's emotional intent. ("My, you look angry.")
—Provide bridges to help a child elaborate intentions in a more organized way; if a child has trouble expressing warmth, say "Come sit in my lap and let's look at this toy."
—When a child seems particularly sad, encourage the child to talk about feelings.
—Explain why you do not want the child to do something.
—Respond in an empathic manner.
—Support a child's understanding of the connection between ideas and feelings.

Practical Tips and Relevant Research

Temperament, Parental Stress, and Depression

When an infant can be regarded as temperamentally difficult, caregivers may need to pay particular attention to their relationship with the parent(s). In research conducted in 1986, Carolyn Cutrona and Beth Troutman of the University of Iowa found that many mothers with difficult infants experience depression and may feel bad about themselves as competent mothers because they cannot comfort their infants. The mothers sometimes develop a love/hate attitude because of the difficulties they experience, and a lingering guilt for those feelings often leads to lowered self-esteem. The researchers recommend setting up a network of supportive people for such mothers so the mothers can realize that they are not to blame for feeling stressed by a demanding baby.

Caregivers who serve difficult babies can use similar supports. Some children will have a strong negative reaction to many things that happen during the day. Good friends and co-workers can help the caregiver deal with the added stress by letting the caregiver talk about it and reminding the caregiver of his or her worth.

The Inconsolable Child

A child who is upset needs time to feel what he or she is feeling and to have a caregiver who expresses understanding and concern. But when the child is inconsolable for a long time (a child who is new to the setting, for example, and is crying for his or her parent), a change of environment will sometimes help the child to move on to better feelings. Taking the child outside or to visit another group of children will often provoke an interest in things around the child. Lowering the lights or singing or playing softly on a musical instrument are other ways of changing the setting to help calm an unhappy child.

Self-esteem: Some Do's and Don'ts

In an article on self-esteem, T. Berry Brazelton, Associate Professor of Pediatrics at Harvard Medical School, states that some actions boost the self-esteem of two- to three-year-olds, while other actions tear it down.[1] Actions or messages that promote self-esteem include letting the child know that you think he or she *can* do something, encouraging the child to finish an activity part way done, and, when necessary, giving only a small amount of help. Children need to hear that mistakes are both okay and part of learning. Reinforcing the child's effort, for example, saying "Good try," also supports the development of the child's self-esteem. Whenever a child accomplishes something on his or her own, be sure to acknowledge the child's accomplishment.

Actions or messages that are destructive to self-esteem include giving negative criticism, especially by belittling or shaming the child, and giving too much praise. Praising the child excessively says to the child you expect him or her to do

---

[1]"The Early Years: How to Raise Your Child's Self-esteem," *Family Circle*, March 3, 1987, 38 and 42.

great things every single time. Emotional abuse (put-downs, verbal attacks, ridicule, and negative labels such as "dumb") is damaging to a child's self-esteem. When the caregiver is always in a bad mood (tense, irritable, humorless), the child will start to feel that there is something wrong with him or her. Finally, a caregiver's withdrawal of love when a child does or does not act a certain way may make the child anxious and insecure.

Caregiver's Practices That Support the Development of Self

The visions listed here are excerpts from Vision VII in *Visions for Infant/Toddler Care: Guidelines for Professional Caregiving* (see also p. 3 in this guide).

Vision: All children need a physically and emotionally secure environment that supports their developing self-knowledge, self-control, and self-esteem and at the same time encourages respect for the feelings and rights of others. Flexibility, responsiveness, and emphasis on individualized care for each infant and toddler are especially important in providing this security. Knowing oneself includes knowing about one's body, feelings, and abilities. It also means identifying oneself as a girl or boy and a member of a family and a larger cultural community. Accepting and taking pride in oneself comes from experiencing success and being accepted by others as unique. Self-esteem develops as children master new abilities, experience success as well as failure, and realize their effectiveness in handling increasingly challenging demands in their own ways in an atmosphere of loving attention.

Practices: The infant/toddler caregiver working in a center or family child care home:

- Treats each child as an individual with his or her own strengths and needs and unique characteristics.
- Recognizes that the caregiver's mood and facial expressions will be seen and felt by the child and will affect the child's experiences and development.
- Helps children who are learning two languages to feel good about themselves as speakers of each language.
- Is sensitive to differing cultural values and expectations concerning independence and expression of feelings.
- Addresses each child by name, talks with each child every day, and encourages each child to call other children and adults by name.
- Has affectionate and appropriate physical contact with each child daily in ways that convey love, affection, and security.
- Helps children through periods of stress, separation, transition, and other crises.
- Gives one-to-one attention to each child.
- Enjoys children and directly expresses the enjoyment to them.
- Delights in each child's success, expresses kindness and support when a child is having trouble, and helps him or her to learn from mistakes.
- Allows each child to comfort himself or herself.
- When possible, offers children choices in activities, materials, and foods and respects their choices.
- Encourages and helps children practice skills when eating, getting dressed, using toys and equipment, cleaning up, and helping others.
- Helps children recognize and accept their feelings—such as joy, affection, anger, jealousy, sadness, fear—and express their feelings in appropriate ways.

- Models the recognition and expression of feelings by naming his or her own feelings while he or she is experiencing those feelings.
- Provides many opportunities for all children, including children with handicapping conditions, to feel effective, experience success, and gain the positive recognition of others.
- Understands the effect of abuse and neglect on children's self-concept and works sensitively with such children.

Vision: *Young infants* [birth to nine months], during the first few weeks and months of their lives, begin to build a sense of self-confidence and security in an environment in which they can trust that an adult will lovingly care for their needs. The adult is someone who feeds the child when the child is hungry, keeps the child warm and comfortable, soothes the child when the child is distressed, and provides interesting things to look at, taste, smell, feel, hear, and touch.

Practices: The caregiver working with *young infants:*

- Listens carefully to an infant's cry and makes decisions quickly and appropriately: allows an infant to cry for only a short time when settling into sleep, comforts an infant who is distressed, or feeds an infant who is hungry.
- Does not substitute food for affection.
- Provides basic physical care (feeding, bathing, dressing, diapering) gently and pleasantly, respecting the tempo and sensitivities of the baby, and talks with the baby during the routines, verbalizing what is being done.
- Holds the infant close, allowing him or her to feel the caregiver's body warmth and heartbeat and to feel comfortable in the adult's arms.
- Creates a personal relationship with each infant and knows the kind of cuddling, stroking, talking, and playing that brings comfort and good feelings to the individual infant.

Vision: For *mobile infants* [six to eighteen months], a loving caregiver provides a home base of warm physical comfort and a safe environment to explore and master. This emotional consistency is essential to developing self-confidence and supporting language, physical, cognitive, and social development.

Practices: The caregiver working with *mobile infants*:

- Helps the exploring infant remove himself or herself from an obstacle that is too frustrating, comforts the child, and supports the child in an alternative activity.
- Recognizes periods when the child has difficulty separating from parents or is fearful of new adults and is supportive of the child.
- Talks to the child frequently about his or her family—where they are, when they will come back, and what they do together.
- Communicates attention and interest, with eyes and voice, to a child who is choosing to explore at a distance from the caregiver.
- Welcomes with a loving voice, hugging, or stroking a child who comes for nurturing.

Vision: *Toddlers* [sixteen to thirty-six months] become aware of many things about themselves, including their separateness from others. A sense of self and growing feelings of independence develop at the same time that toddlers realize the importance of parents and other caregivers. The healthy toddler's inner world is filled with conflicting feelings and ideas: independence and dependence, confidence and doubt, fear and power, hostility and love, anger and tenderness, aggression and passivity. The wide range of toddlers' feelings and actions challenges the resourcefulness and knowledge of the adults who provide emotional security.

Practices: The caregiver working with *toddlers*:

- Supports the child's developing awareness of himself or herself as a member of a family and of an ethnic or social group by talking about families, using photographs, mirrors, or other appropriate objects, and by celebrating cultural events with children.
- Uses books, pictures, stories, and discussion to help children identify positively with the events and experiences of their lives, such as divorce, moving, single-parent families, extended families, or birth of siblings.
- Provides opportunities for toddlers to learn to help themselves, such as taking off jackets or pouring juice, and shares children's pleasure in new skills.
- Responds with sympathetic attention to the toddler's intense feelings of love, joy, loneliness, anger, and disappointment.
- Helps the toddler to understand his or her own feelings and to express feelings in acceptable ways.
- Understands and supports the toddler's need to assert his or her autonomy when, for example, the toddler may say no or "me do it" to the caregiver.
- Understands that toddlers will alternate between needing to assert a desire for independence one minute and needing to be dependent on the caregiver (whining, climbing on lap, bringing toys to show, needing assistance) the next minute.

the Program for infant toddler caregivers

Section Two: The Development of Social Skills

Introduction

In the first paper in this section, J. Ronald Lally describes a basic caregiving approach called the responsive process. The caregiver's role is defined as a combination of learner, provider, and adapter. The responsive process helps develop the kind of nurturing relationships that lead young children to feel secure in themselves, value others, and learn acceptable behavior. In his paper Dr. Lally points out the need for caregivers to redefine their roles in the development of the child's self and social behavior as children grow from young infants to mobile infants to toddlers.

J. Ronald Lally is Director of the Center for Child and Family Studies, Far West Laboratory for Educational Research and Development in San Francisco, which created The Program for Infant/Toddler Caregivers for the California State Department of Education. The caregiver training system is based on videos, written materials, and technical assistance. Dr. Lally is coauthor with Ira Gordon of *Learning Games for Infants and Toddlers;* coauthor with Alice Honig of *Infant Caregiving: A Design for Training;* and coauthor with Kuno Beller, Ira Gordon, and Leon Yarrow of *Studies in Socio-Emotional Development in Infancy.* Dr. Lally also directed the Syracuse University Family Development Research Program, an early intervention program (from birth to age five) with low-income children and their families, and is currently directing the longitudinal follow-up study of the effects of the Syracuse program.

In the second paper, Jeree H. Pawl describes as gifts ten particular ways of interacting with infants and toddlers. The ten gifts illustrate the types of caregiver behaviors that directly influence infant self-esteem and model for the child how best to relate socially to other human beings.

Jeree H. Pawl is Associate Clinical Professor, Department of Psychiatry, School of Medicine, University of California, San Francisco, and Acting Director of the Infant-Parent Program of the UCSF at San Francisco General Hospital. Before moving to San Francisco, Dr. Pawl worked with Dr. Selma Fraiberg at the University of Michigan Medical School. Dr. Pawl is an expert in the assessment and treatment of developing relationships of infants, toddlers, and their parents. Currently, she is the editor of *Zero to Three: Bulletin of the National Center for Clinical Infant Programs* and serves on that organization's Board of Directors. In addition, she serves on the Board of Directors of several organizations concerned with the development and supportive treatment of families with infants and toddlers. Her most recent publications and research focus primarily on child abuse and prevention and preventive intervention with anxiously attached infants.

Social Skills: Vision Statement

The caregiver helps each child feel accepted in the group, assists children in learning to communicate and get along with others, and encourages feelings of empathy and mutual respect among children and adults.

To develop social skills needed to work and play cooperatively and productively, children must feel secure themselves and value others. While nurturing each child's own self-esteem, caregivers should promote and model interactions that assist children in learning to get along with others and encourage feelings of empathy and mutual respect.

Young infants [birth to nine months] enter the world with a capacity and a need for social contact. Infants need both protective and stimulating social interactions with a few familiar, caring adults who get to know the children as individuals; use frequent eye contact; play responsive social games; and talk to the children during feeding, bathing, and dressing. The adults' understanding response to the infants' signals increases the infants' participation in social interactions and their ability to read the signals of others.

Mobile infants [six to eighteen months] are curious about others but need assistance and supervision in interacting with other children. They continue to need one or a few adults on a consistent basis as their most important social partner(s).

Toddlers' [sixteen to thirty-six months] social awareness is much more complex than that of younger children. Toddlers can begin to understand that others have feelings, too—sometimes similar to and sometimes different from their own. They imitate many of the social behaviors of other children and adults: taking turns with a ball, sharing a game, putting toys away. As toddlers become increasingly interested in other children, they continue to rely on familiar adults to guide and support their interactions.

This statement is an excerpt from Vision VII, Development of Each Child's Competence—Social and Emotional Development, in *Visions for Infant/Toddler Care: Guidelines for Professional Caregiving* (Sacramento: California State Department of Education, 1988). The *Visions* document outlines the visions or goals of The Program for Infant/Toddler Caregivers.

Creating Nurturing Relationships with Infants and Toddlers

J. Ronald Lally

For infants and toddlers to prosper in group care, caregivers have to form sensitive and responsive relationships with each child individually. Such relationships are important to children of all ages but particularly so to infants and toddlers. Your sensitivity and responsiveness as a caregiver strongly influence how each child in your care will act toward and feel about the other people around him or her. If you as the caregiver are reasonably responsive to the baby's message, when the baby cries, you come; when the baby acts shyly, you do not force the baby to make contact. You can give a positive tint to the lens through which the child looks at life.

Your responsive behavior as a caregiver has the following effects:

- The child learns at a young age that he or she can have an effect on the outside world and can make things happen.

- The child is encouraged to send more messages, to keep reaching out. The child will use and sharpen his or her communication skills because the child learns that communication works.
- The child builds self-esteem, learning, "I am someone who is paid attention to—I am worthy."
- The child's feelings of security, trust, and confidence in the world are nurtured.

Caregivers can learn to be more responsive by getting in the habit of following a three-step responsive process. These three steps blend into a natural "dance" that both the child and caregiver enjoy.

The Responsive Process

The three steps in the responsive process are *watch*, *ask*, and *adapt*.

Step One: Watch

Try to see the world in the way that a particular infant sees it. Do everything possible that will help you see life through the infant's eyes and feel life through the infant's skin.

Begin your interactions with any infant or toddler by simply watching the child. By watching first and not just rushing to do things for the baby, you can avoid the mistake of reacting before you receive the full message from the child. Look with both eyes. Listen with both ears. Give the child time to get his or her message across. Watch for both verbal and nonverbal messages.

Try to get in the habit of constantly gauging the child's actions. Pay attention to all the channels of communication that are available to babies. Watch how they curl their toes, arch their backs, widen their eyes, wave their arms, grow quiet. With older children watch their many gestures. For example, if children tug at their hair, sit apart from other children, or lie curled toward the wall, they are probably experiencing fear. You will be surprised at how much you can learn by watching.

In your daily contacts with an infant or toddler, you need to remember that *you must be willing to choose the role of learner* for part of the time. Only by first learning from the infant or toddler what he or she is calling for can you choose the right response.

Being a learner means spending a lot of your time observing, "reading" the child, figuring out what message he or she is sending—not only the sounds and words but also the facial expressions, hand gestures, and other body language. Sometimes learning means getting right down on the floor with the child and seeing things as the child sees them.

By observing the child you will see things that require your immediate attention, such as signs of physical discomfort or hunger. You will also get to know the child; you will find out over time what the child's special interests and preferences are and how you can build on those interests to establish a nurturing relationship. By being willing to pay close attention, by making this kind of observation part of your caregiving style, you will also discover the child's particular temperamental traits—how active or shy the child appears to be, what kind of attention span the child has, how adaptable to new things the child is.

Until you are willing to assume the role of watcher while you are relating to young children, you will continually do things with and for children that are inappropriate, inaccurate, and sometimes emotionally harmful. Being willing to

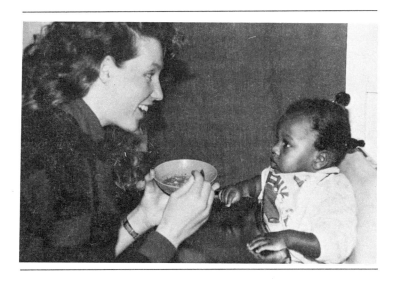

take on the role of observer is no guarantee that you will always make the right moves with a child. But because you are paying attention to the messages of the child, you will quickly discover what is not working and can try something else.

Step Two: Ask

After watching for a while, step back into your adult role and ask yourself how you might set up the environment—the emotional, intellectual, and physical climate, the social setting, and your personal behavior—in ways that will assist the child the most.

When you begin each new encounter with a child, allow for the possibility that you may not know what the child likes or is like on that day. Ask the child with your movements and your words. Magda Gerber, the Director of Resources for Infant Educarers and one of the most highly respected trainers in the field of infant care, says we should take this role of asking very seriously:

I go so far as asking the baby, the two-week-old baby or younger, "I see you seem unhappy. What can I do? I don't know what makes you unhappy, but I want to learn it." I think by asking, you invite the baby to give you the answer and be a partner.

Ask yourself: What messages is the child sending? What are the emotional parts to the message—the intellectual, the physical, and so forth? For example, you see that the child seems really to enjoy playing with toy cars. You guess that one way to engage or relate to the child might be through joint play with cars. One way to ask the question is to introduce cars to the relationship and see what happens. Also ask yourself: What message am I sending? What am I bringing to this relationship?

Sometimes you do not get a child's message because your own feelings get in the way, causing you to misread or simply not see and hear what is really happening. Part of tuning in to another person's emotional messages is being aware of your own feelings and emotional states. The more clearly you understand what is going on inside you, the more likely you will be able to read and respond appropriately to a child's signals.

As the caregiver you need to ask yourself about two kinds of feelings, those of the present moment and those from the past:

1. The feelings of the present moment include your level of energy and your mood. Are you feeling tired, tense, irritable, or in good spirits? It is important to check in with yourself about such feelings and to realize that you are continually communicating them. Children are so sensitive to the adults with whom they interact that they pick up easily on feeling and tone.
2. The feelings from the past are more complicated because they come from your own childhood experiences. Often those emotional patterns continue to influence you as an adult even though you are not aware of the fact. If the past emotions are not acknowledged, they may interfere with your ability to read a child's

messages clearly and may even cause you to respond in inappropriate or harmful ways.

Becoming aware of how emotional experiences from the past affect your behavior in the present is an ongoing process that takes practice. Just by being willing to look at the connections between past feelings and events and present experience, you will bring a new awareness to your work. The following example shows what a caregiver named Carol learned about herself when she was willing to ask herself about the connections between her past and present experience:

Carol began to notice that she was bothered by a child who had a tendency to tease the younger children, provoking them and taking away their toys. She also noticed how intensely the child's actions irritated and angered her. She could not stand the way the boy acted. She saw that increasingly her interactions with the child left her feeling upset, worn out, and defeated—and she blamed the child.

Rather than leave things that way, Carol looked inward. Reflecting on her own childhood, Carol remembered how she had felt when her older brother used to tease and torment her by taking her toys away and hiding them—how her brother would laugh at her protests. When she turned to her mother to intervene, her mother most often would tell her to work it out herself. Carol experienced again those feelings of frustration, pain, and anger that had come over her when she had to deal with the situation as a child.

Sometimes, untangling your intense emotional reactions to a child or to a particular kind of behavior in children is very difficult. At such times you should ask for help from another caregiver or a supervisor. Another's view of the situation may shed light on "blind spots" and "hot spots" you carry with you from your own childhood.

When Carol became aware that emotional responses from the past were getting in the way of her care of the child, her feelings about the child began to change. She asked another caregiver to observe her and the child and to offer suggestions about different ways she might handle the situation. She found that second view very helpful. She realized that her current feeling of intense anger limited her ability to provide the child with constructive choices and had more to do with her than with the child.

Instead of being overwhelmed and upset in the face of the child's provocative behavior, Carol began to focus much more clearly on what was happening in the present with the young teaser and to devise strategies for action.

To be a sensitive caregiver you need to learn about yourself as well as the children you serve. Your emotional reactions to different children and to certain behaviors are a big part of your care. Look inward and consider your feelings. Knowing your "hot spots" and "blind spots" makes you a better caregiver.

Step Three: Adapt

While you continue to watch and ask, engage the child. As you engage the child, you will collect valuable information. You may learn that the child does not like to share but does like to show things to you or uses objects to establish closer contact with you. You may find that the child wants to be left alone. Adapt your actions in accordance with what you learn: leave, show interest in what the child shows you, or allow the child to get on your lap because he or she seems to be asking for that.

Your action does not have to be in direct relation to the child. You may act on the environment to make it more interesting to the child—for example, put more objects on the floor—or you may

try to interest some other children in peer contact. The point of your actions, however, should always be linked to your reading of the child.

Watch carefully how the child responds to the conditions you have set up and the actions you have taken. Then modify the conditions or actions based on what you learn from the child's responses. Continue to learn and make adjustments until you feel you are providing what the child needs.

The role of adapter is the most creative part of your relationship with infants and toddlers. You need to look at the child's reaction to the hug you gave, the question you asked, the activities you set up, the decision you made to leave the child alone to see how he or she handled things—and adapt your subsequent actions based on the messages the child sent out in response to what you provided. Ask the questions: How close was I in my original guess about what this child needed? What is the message now? How should I change my behavior, revise the environment, or alter my opinions about this child based on what the child is telling me and on what he or she needs? How must I change conditions or my actions so that what I provide better meets the needs of this child?

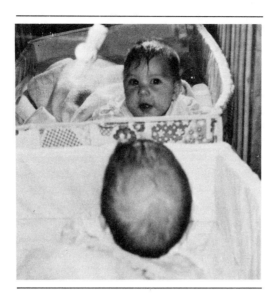

Adaptation and Age

One reason continued adaptation by caregivers is important is that infants change so quickly. The ways in which you provide the care will change as the child grows from infancy to toddlerhood: you will move more into the background as the child becomes more competent to provide for himself or herself.

Adapting to the Needs of Young Infants

The very young infant who is not yet crawling usually needs you to provide care in a physical way by bringing things to him or her—food, a clean diaper, objects to hold or suck—or by taking him or her to sights, sounds, and people, out in the sun, or next to a couple of toddlers. The infant also needs consistent loving contact with you—to see your face, hear your reassuring voice, feel the warm skin-to-skin contact—so the infant can feel confident that someone is there who will provide for his or her needs. Exactly how you go about doing that for a particular infant depends on the things you learn about the child in your day-to-day use of the responsive process.

Adapting to the Needs of Mobile Infants

The crawler, new walker, or young toddler, because he or she is able to move about, can often go after what he or she wants. The child can come to you, go to food, and avoid things that are unpleasant. The young mover needs a caregiver who provides opportunities to experiment and take risks in an environment that is safe, interesting, and healthful. At this developmental stage you are not bringing the child to things or things to the child as often as you did with the younger child. Instead you are arranging or creating environments and possibilities that allow interesting things to happen.

Your role is to set things up in the young mover's environment to make it safe and easy to explore. In that way you are automatically giving many confidence-building messages. When the environment is not ordered with the "mover" in mind, the usual caregiver message is very different: "Don't explore. Don't do things you choose because I do not have confidence that you won't get hurt or destroy things." The specific experiences and the kinds of environments you provide particular children must grow out of your careful observations as you interact with the children.

Emotional availability is also important here. At this age the child often likes the caregiver to be available but not intrusive. You may have had an experience with a waitress whose eyes avoided your table so you would not be able to call her over. Sometimes you may withhold your full presence from children in the same way, afraid that being completely accessible will use you up or perhaps spoil the child. But you cannot read the child's signals or provide appropriate reassuring contact without attending to the child. So be generous with your attention. Unlike the inattentive waitress, let frequent eye checks say to the child, "If you want me, you've got me."

Think how wonderful and emotionally settling the knowledge is to the mobile infant to look up and see that you are there if needed. When your eyes meet those of the child and you send messages of love and reassurance across the room, you are providing just the message the child is looking for. The unspoken messages you give to a child, "I'm here if you need me" and "I'm proud of your exploration," help to instill the confidence that the early toddler usually requires. What the child gets through this kind of emotional interaction is reassurance not only of the materials of growth (food, a safe and interesting environment, hugs) but also of your willingness to let the child choose and explore on his or her own: "I have confidence in your competence."

Adapting to the Needs of Older Infants

The older infant with good language and movement skills has the ability for abstract thought. Here your role shifts focus again. For your relationship to work, you have to understand that at this age the child is not only learning about the many choices available to him or her but also coming to understand that individual responsibility comes along

with choice. The whole notion of individuality becomes central to the older infant's development. Having mastered walking, climbing, and combining words, the older infant begins to develop fantasy in thought and language as well as a feeling for past and future.

The child at this stage of development may see others as a barrier to getting what he or she wants but also begins to see the positive side of cooperation. The older infant often shows his or her developing sense of self by resisting others or saying no. The infant also takes pride in his or her own creations. The child needs a relationship with a provider who will support his or her curiosity, independent action, and creativity. At the same time the child needs tactful help to see how his or her curiosity, creativity, and independent action affect the people the child shares space with as well as the environment and other living things. You as the caregiver become a kind of sounding board by letting the child bounce off you his or her growing sense of what is acceptable or unacceptable. With the right sounding board, the child's creativity, curiosity, and independence continue to blossom while the child learns that he or she may not pour milk into the sandbox, destroy toys, or hurt other children.

The Evolution of Responsive Care

The more the steps of the responsive process (watch, ask, adapt) are practiced, the more responsive the caregiver becomes with the child.

Somewhat Responsive Care

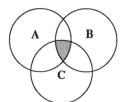

More Responsive Care

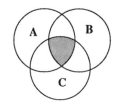

Responsive Care

A—WATCH   B—ASK   C—ADAPT

The process of watching, asking, and adapting—the core of a good caregiver–infant relationship—happens hundreds of times a day. When you are truly tuned in to the children you serve, the process becomes second nature. You realize that watching, asking, and adapting are always interconnected in the daily give-and-take of caregiver-infant relationships. Once you understand the process, you blend the three steps into a natural dance that both partners enjoy.

Tips for Getting in Tune

1. Be attentively respectful. Observe without interfering. Spend time quietly looking and listening—leaving the child's psychological space intact—without interrupting or breaking into the child's activity.

2. Be an asker. Ask the child through words and actions what is right for him or her: "I wonder what is motivating Meg?" "I wonder what Joe is interested in this morning?" Ask yourself: Is what I'm doing meeting the child's needs?

3. Pay attention to your own feelings. Gauge the part your feelings play in the relationship.

4. Keep in mind your own special emotional inclinations—your "hot spots" and "blind spots."

5. Watch as you act. When you take an action, watch while you do it and do not go too fast. Give the baby time to show you a response that you can learn something from.

6. See behind the action. Do not just see an action or behavior but see the reason and emotion behind the action. When an older infant scribbles on the wall, for example, he or she may be so consumed with trying out the new line-making skill that the infant may feel the act of making lines on any surface should be rewarded.

7. Use the information you have learned about children and child care—how children develop, how to cope with cultural differences, how to set up environments, how to use materials to assist you in the adaptation process.

8. Pay special attention to what you have already learned from your interactions with each child in your care.

9. Use all the information artistically to create a unique exchange with each child.

Self-esteem, Security, and Social Competence: Ten Caregiving Gifts

Jeree H. Pawl

Caregivers take on a big responsibility when they care for very young children for long periods of time outside the children's homes. The caregiver is expected to be a competent and affectionate extension of the child's parents. The child learns to turn to the caregiver to meet his or her basic emotional needs. The caregiver has great influence over the picture the child begins to form of the world around him or her—that is, the child's impression of how he or she will be treated and how he or she should act around others. In instances in which the infant's or toddler's relationship with his or her own parent is inadequate, the caregiver's contribution to that child's sense of self and of the world is beyond measure.

Ten Caregiving Gifts

In this paper I present ten suggestions for care that I believe are some of the most powerful ways a caregiver can support infants, toddlers, and their parents. I call these *caregiving gifts* because of the great benefits infants and toddlers gain in self-esteem, security, and social competence.

Gift One: Respond to Very Young Infants in Ways That Encourage Them to Feel They Can Make Things Happen

The first gift the caregiver can give an infant is to respond in a way that encourages the infant to feel he or she has an impact on the world—that he or she can make something happen. Adults often are miserable at those times when they feel least competent, least effective, and most helpless. Babies are helpless in many ways—they are immobile and cannot fend for themselves—but they can let the caregiver know that they have a need. When the baby's communication of need brings a prompt and caring response, preferably from someone familiar, the response gives the baby the experience of having an effect, a sense of power.

The caregiver needs to respond when the need is expressed, not when the time is convenient or better fits the caregiver's schedule. Imagine how good babies feel when the giants come running. Small and helpless as babies are, they can command and control what they need. Early infancy is not the time when adults need to teach children the limits of their ability to cause things to happen. Just the opposite. By helping the young infant gain a sense of

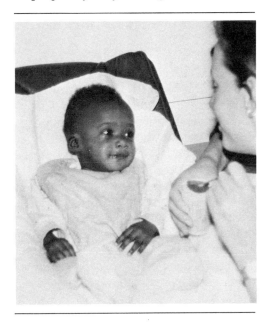

helping the young infant gain a sense of being able to cause things to happen, the caregiver creates a feeling of power in the infant and a beginning confidence in the child's sense of self.

Thus when a baby expresses a need for food, the caregiver feeds the baby but does more than satisfy the baby's hunger. The caregiver gives himself or herself as a responder. The baby begins to trust that the caregiver is there for the baby, to expect the caregiver to be there, and to experience the pleasure in being able to get the caregiver to respond to the baby's needs.

Gift Two: Help Young Infants Learn They Have Ways to Take Care of Their Own Needs

The pleasure a child experiences in getting the caregiver to respond to his or her needs leads to the next caregiver's gift. If the caregiver always does things for a baby, the child will not have a chance to learn about his or her own competence. Therefore, another kind of power caregivers can offer to babies and toddlers is the power to learn that they also have ways to take care of themselves.

When a baby is mildly distressed—dry, not hungry but "fussy"—the caregiver can speak to the baby (can the baby use sounds to comfort himself or herself?), pat the baby briefly (can the baby pat himself or herself?), and sometimes reposition the child. Perhaps with this cooperation the baby will find out that with the knees up he or she feels more content, or that while on the tummy the baby can find his or her own thumb. Next time the baby might move to that position without help. The baby learns that he or she can rely on things directly under his or her control. Again, the baby feels effective and competent.

This cooperation between the caregiver (as an alert and sensitive extension of the baby) and the baby (who can

manage some things without help) underlies the growing sense of competence that is so necessary to the child's development of self-esteem. Many day-to-day experiences contribute to that complex sense, but it surely begins with caregivers both responding to babies' needs and providing babies with opportunities to experience being able to take care of themselves.

The process only works, of course, if the child's ability to care for himself or herself is within the child's capacity. Otherwise, the child is overwhelmed, disorganized, and helpless. Here the art of caregiving comes in: When do I help? How much should I help? When should I let the infant do things on his or her own? Occasionally, no matter what the caregiver does, a baby will experience helplessness and frustration. But if caregivers meet babies where they need help and let babies do what they can, the babies will experience an overall sense of control and confidence as a result.

One obvious way to promote a sense of competence is to offer choices to the toddler. That does not mean turning endless difficult decisions over to the child: "Do you want to look at a book, play on the slide, play with a puzzle, paint, or rest?" Promoting competence does mean listening to and granting the child his or her preference ("Go outside"). As the young child increasingly shows the interest and ability to make choices, promoting a sense of competence means increasing the opportunities for choice.

The caregiver may provide opportunities by setting up the home or center so that a variety of play choices is available. When a child can move from one activity to another, depending on his or her mood and interest, the child will have a continuing sense of control over himself or herself, the environment, and the expression of himself or herself in the environment.

Gift Three: Help Infants and Toddlers Develop Confidence and Trust in Others

At the same time the baby is experiencing an emerging self-assurance, he or she also is developing a complementary sense of confidence in others. The baby is learning to trust that his or her needs will be noticed and that the world will respond. So, along with the positive sense of self, the baby develops the sense of trust in the caregiver. Trust is essential to how the baby feels about what he or she can expect from people in the world: Will people help? Will they hurt? Will they just not notice? Should I trust people? Can I trust myself?

When the caregiver pays close attention to an infant's need to trust self or another, the caregiver is not only satisfying the child's hunger or lessening the discomfort but also creating a confidence with the infant in self, others, and the way the world behaves. That confidence is far more meaningful than the momentary satisfaction of hunger.

Astonishingly quickly, a baby begins to have expectations about what will happen when a need is expressed—who will do what to whom. Caregiver–child interactions work best for babies when the baby can begin to *predict* what will happen. For that to occur, the events must

be familiar. The baby must be cared for in a consistent setting and get used to where things are and when things usually happen. When the baby is cared for by the same few people for months at a time, the baby becomes familiar with how the caregiver will treat him or her.

Babies can adapt to different caregiver styles but not endlessly so without considerable cost. Each caregiver:

- Has his or her own personal style.
- Picks up a baby differently from anyone else.
- Picks up different babies differently.
- Has his or her own unique voice, smell, and rhythms.
- Is faster or slower, more vigorous or gentle than another.

Babies learn to anticipate those circumstances very rapidly. Within days babies recognize the caregiver's smell, face, and voice.

If a total shift of caregivers occurs, babies as young as two months of age demonstrate their distress by having feeding and sleeping problems. To some extent the distress can be understood as a reaction to the disruption of the babies' ability to predict what will happen—they do not know what to expect. This example illustrates the problem:

> The disruption is like learning to dance perfectly with one partner and then suddenly being confronted with another. The steps you know do not work—the new partner is kicking you in the leg and it feels awful. Your sense of control, the ability to predict your part in the dance is badly damaged. You feel insecure and are not even sure if you can dance at all.

If you face an endless stream of new partners, you may learn to dance with all of them, but you will always have to let them lead, and the lovely integration of partners will not be possible to achieve. In contrast, a dance with the same partner every time is personalized and intimate.

The caregiver predicts the baby's response just as the baby predicts the caregiver's:

Two sets of eyebrows are raised almost simultaneously, a smile begins on one face, broadens on the other, the lips are pursed, the other smiles and bursts into laughter. Then the partner's lips are pursed again and the dance continues.

The imitations, the leads in even so small an exchange as a series of smiles and mouth movements are most meaningful. The wonderful ability of a caregiver to keep his or her face endlessly interesting and responsive to the slightest variation in the baby's cues is an internal, unconscious response. But the response is based on the intimate knowledge of the baby, on the ability to know without thinking what the next right move is.

Gift Four: Help Babies Learn About Intimacy

Intimacy or closeness between infant and caregiver can develop only when

both have enough time together to know each other well. Babies are always ready for closeness, but they need a caregiver or at most two or three caregivers who know them, who like them, and who are principally responsible for their care. *More than three caregivers taxes the very young child and dilutes the quality and depth of the baby's relationships.*

Caregivers help babies develop the ability to engage in intimate interactions when caregivers do not stretch babies beyond their limits. The fewer the caregivers with whom a baby must learn to "dance," the safer the baby is from having his or her ability for intimacy overtaxed. Caregiving programs should ensure that no one caregiver has more than three young infants for whom he or she is the principal caregiver and that the infants are almost always the same infants. This practice will preserve the infant's capacity for closeness and intimacy, a capacity that affects everything that makes a baby feel effective, competent, and in tune with the caregiver.

Ordinary caregiving routines are special opportunities for closeness. These include:

- Welcoming a child in the morning
- Feeding, diapering, cleaning the face and hands
- Putting a child down and getting the child up from a nap
- Getting a child dressed
- Preparing a child to go home

Routines are not tasks to be rushed through but moments when the child learns that the caregiver knows and respects the child's likes, dislikes, moods, and fears. The caregiver's actions lay the foundation for a lifetime of such communication. Nothing could be more important.

Gift Five: Help Toddlers Learn That Adults Cannot Solve Every Problem

For the toddler as well as the younger infant, it is equally important to have a caregiver who is intimate and trustworthy, who knows the child well, and who provides for that child individually. The toddler stage is also the time, however, for the caregiver to move from readily meeting the child's needs to helping the child see that he or she has some desires that the caregiver cannot and will not satisfy. The caregiver can expect the toddler gradually to show increased tolerance for delay and for the caregiver's inability at times to gratify the toddler's demands and wishes. An important caregiver role is to recognize and take full advantage of the toddler's rapidly developing capacity to accept the caregiver's limits to meet all the toddler's desires.

It is vital for toddlers to learn that adults do not have the power to make the world perfect. Sometimes caregivers can help toddlers appreciate adults' limits more easily than parents. Caregivers are far freer than parents from the powerful, passionate attachment to the child that sometimes pushes parents to present themselves as persons who can solve any problem and always make the child happy. If they could, many parents would create a world for their child where everything was good and where joy, happiness, and contentment were the only emotions experienced.

Sometimes caregivers may lean in that direction, too. For the caregiver who feels that way and sends that message, a great tangle of emotions occurs when a child sees the caregiver as a source of unhappiness. What the child wants may be unreasonable and yet the child behaves as if the caregiver is deliberately cruel. In such a situation, the following may result:

1. If the caregiver feels that he or she *should* make everything all right and cannot, the caregiver feels guilty. That makes the caregiver angry and soon what should be a simple "No, I'm sorry" is an angry no or worse.

2. If the caregiver changes his or her mind along the way and lets the toddler have what the caregiver's judgment says the toddler should not have, the caregiver runs the danger of agreeing with the child that the caregiver is the source of all pleasure and displeasure. By doing so the caregiver supports rather than weakens the child's notion that if the child feels bad it is the caregiver's fault and the caregiver could fix it if he or she wanted to. *It is vital that children learn that the caregiver cannot make everything all right.*

What is needed in this situation is another kind of dance, one slightly different from the dance with younger infants. The dance now shows the child that the caregiver will still give what is possible but that the caregiver cannot give everything—and some things the caregiver should not give at all. There is a gradual caregiving transition from the role of principal provider to a role that helps the toddler see that he or she, too, has some responsibility for his or her own feelings. This gift must be given sensitively so that the caregiver does not expect too much too soon and the toddler does not feel suddenly abandoned.

Gift Six: Be Tolerant of Toddlers' Internal Conflicts and Desires

As infants move into toddlerhood, they want and demand many things that are harmful or dangerous or totally impossible. Caregivers occasionally frustrate some powerful wishes and are called on to satisfy the unsatisfiable. How caregivers understand and feel about those situations matters as much as the child's behavior does. The caregiver's feelings are quickly and easily sensed by the toddler, and the message the toddler receives about how the caregiver evaluates him or her at those times is extremely important to the toddler's development.

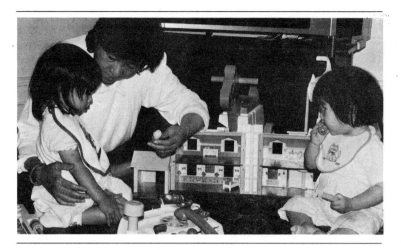

The toddler may express internal conflicts and desires:

I will be big. I will be small. I will be bigsmall!

I want orange—no grape—no orange—no grape—no orange—no strawberry.

It is easy to get caught up in this internal conflict, for instance, by fetching a series of drinks for the grumpy toddler, none of which does the trick. The drinks do not help because the toddler wants them all—some magical, multicolored drink that will fix the toddler's bad feelings. But those feelings really have nothing to do with drinks, multicolored or otherwise.

At such a time the caregiver needs to recognize the child's dilemma, sympathize with it, stop the futile attempts to please, and offer a hug—essentially calling a halt to efforts to please. If the toddler refuses all juice, fine; the caregiver accepts the child's control cheerfully. If the child flings himself or herself on the floor, the caregiver offers sympathy and comfort but does not get plugged in to the child's tantrum. If the caregiver can recognize, for example, that a certain toddler is out of sorts and that the toddler's insistence on having another cupcake is not really about cupcakes at all, the caregiver can offer that child comfort instead of exasperation.

The following example illustrates the importance of accepting and allowing the child's feelings:

When Sally wants to explore the record player that was brought in to play music for dancing, she has a fit when the caregiver stops her. The caregiver can admire Sally's curiosity and acknowledge that her wish to explore the record player and how it works is splendid. The caregiver can tell Sally that she knows Sally wants to play with the record player and that of course Sally is grumpy when she cannot. The caregiver will not expect the child always to take such things graciously. Most importantly, the caregiver allows Sally to *own her feelings*.

By accepting and allowing feelings even as caregivers control a child's behavior, caregivers really help the toddler.

Gift Seven: Help Toddlers Sort Out the Evaluations of Adults

When toddlers are angry and unhappy, it is often hard for the caregiver to acknowledge, without feeling defensive and guilty, either that he or she has caused the anger and unhappiness or that the toddlers blame the caregiver for causing those emotions. Many times, because of the caregiver's discomfort, he or she wants the child to drop the issue quickly and be good-natured. The caregiver wishes that the toddler would stop expressing the pain and unhappiness the toddler feels because the behavior offers continuing evidence that the toddler feels wronged. At such times both the toddler and the caregiver will benefit if the caregiver can sort out the feelings for the child.

The earlier example of Sally and the record player shows that Sally needs to know just what she has been told she should not do and what part of her action is all right with the caregiver. Too often all of the child's behavior is treated as one problem: the curiosity, the disappointment and anger, and the resulting behavior are not separated. With that kind of reaction from the caregiver, Sally is being asked to give up not only all her actions but also her feelings. As far as she knows, the feeling of curiosity that prompted her contact with the record player was bad, her unhappiness was bad, and her grumpy behavior was bad. When the caregiver points out to Sally exactly what part of the bundle of behaviors and feelings will not be allowed and what is all right, Sally feels better. Through word and action the caregiver communicates:

> I think it is good for you to be curious. And it is natural for you to feel disappointed or angry when your curiosity is stifled. I want you to love your curiosity and treasure it as I do and know that it is all right with me if you feel disappointed or angry. What you cannot do is touch the record player while it is playing or kick me because I stop you from touching the record player.

When a caregiver does this kind of sensitive sorting out, he or she gives the child another precious gift. And the gift often makes the caregiver's own job easier because the child does not have so many things to be frustrated about. The sorting out:

1. Helps the child handle and tolerate feelings.
2. Helps the child learn what his or her feelings are.

By naming feelings, accepting feelings, and never demanding that children not feel them or not have some way to express them, caregivers create a mentally healthy environment for growth.

Gift Eight: Match Your Reaction to the Temperament of the Baby

Review the lessons from the earlier paper in this guide, "Temperaments of Infants and Toddlers," by Stella Chess. Because the topic was covered well, I will not repeat the lessons except to say that accepting rather than trying to change a young child's temperament is central to the caregiver's role in building the child's self-esteem.

Gift Nine: Exchange Information with Parents About Their Children

Continuity of care is important to the emotional security of both infants and toddlers. This continuity is helped by the careful exchange of information about the child's development, the child's mood and behavior, and significant things that happened to the child. Also relevant is what kind of day the child has had leading up to the moment of exchange of responsibility. Taking the time to share the information ensures continuity of understanding and forges the quality of relationship between parent and caregiver that the child needs.

The exchange of information works both ways. For example, a parent can let the caregiver know that Susie really did not want to come to the program today because no one could find her favorite doll that morning. The caregiver's awareness of Susie's feelings when she arrives promises to make a much better day for both the child and the caregiver.

Gift Ten: Remind Children in Child Care of the Absent Parents' Continued Existence

There should be ready reminders for children in child care of their parents' continued existence. Pictures, items from home, and conversation about absent parents contribute to the children's sense of security about their parents' guaranteed return. For children who have trouble with the switch in care from caregiver to parent, caregivers can help by discussing when the parents will come and what the child might do to engage the parent ("Look what I made!").

Talking with the parent also ensures a less abrupt shift. The caregiver can help the parent understand the meaning of the behavior of the child so that a sensitive parent will not misinterpret the behavior. The following example illustrates a caregiver's response to a difficult transition:

> "Billy has really been missing you today and is giving you the cold shoulder so you'll be sure to get the message." The caregiver may suggest that the parent say, "I really wondered what you were doing today, Billy. When you're ready, I'll be right here and we can go." That gives Billy time

to wrestle with his feelings, gives him control, and offers a way to approach his parent when he is ready.

This kind of help with transitions can avoid a lot of misunderstanding, hurt feelings, and perhaps the beginning of a bad evening. In addition, a sensitive response to the child having difficulty with transitions contributes to the child's sense of trust, security, and importance.

Conclusion

The caregiver who creates an atmosphere and a relationship with infants and toddlers in which the children are helped to feel effective, trusting, mutually engaged with the caregiver, personally known and understood, and the proper owner of their own wishes and feelings gives an enormous gift to the children and their parents. With this gift the children's emotional security and self-esteem will develop naturally. Caring for such children will be easier and more pleasurable. The caregivers will see the evidence of their dedication, understanding, and hard work in the healthy emotional development of the children in their care. There could be no better reward.

Practical Tips and Relevant Research

Getting in Tune

We have suggested throughout this guide that caregivers "get in tune," "be in rhythm," "get on the same wavelength," and "dance" with the infant or toddler. Sometimes caregivers can try too hard. Evelyn Thoman gives some good advice in her book, *Born Dancing: The Relaxed Parents' Guide to Making Babies Smart with Love*. The following is a summary of that advice:

- Accept from the start that you will make mistakes. You will do things that are "out of tune"—everyone does. Do not be down on yourself. Instead, try to learn from the mistakes.
- Forget about trying to find the one way to do things or the simple answer that will work in most circumstances. Expect that there will be times when you are confused and uncertain about what to do. Starting from that uncertainty with each child instead of from a set way of doing things will actually help you to learn a great deal about the child.
- Changes in children, shifts in mood, and day-to-day situations influence how your daily relationships will go. Try to get away from thinking in terms of absolutes—good and bad, right and wrong, good-natured and cranky. The truth about the child is always less definite than that.

Relating Day to Day

Something as simple as the way a caregiver reacts to a child's gaze can have an impact on a child's emotional development. What makes the difference is not the one reaction but the day-in-and-day-out style of reacting to the gaze and all the other seemingly insignificant contacts with a young child.

For a two-year period, Daniel Stern of the Cornell Medical School in New York City collected videotapes of infants and their mothers engaged in normal everyday activities. He believes that the small give-and-take interactions of daily life between caregivers and infants can shape the way children relate to people later in life. Dr. Stern believes that children's personalities are influenced more in day-to-day encounters with caregivers than in the so-called critical periods of development. What happens in infancy can be changed throughout life by those same day-to-day interactions or by therapy. He does believe, however, that early interactions, though not critical, set the stage for the way children expect relationships to go.

Of great importance in the development of personality is the way a caregiver reacts to a very young child's show of will. Take the child's gaze as an example. When a baby breaks eye contact, the baby often is giving the message that he or she has had enough contact. If the caregiver pursues the gaze and forces contact, he or she, without even knowing it, might be teaching the child that the caregiver's will rather than the child's will is more important and that the caregiver, not the child, has the right to display power.

Dr. Stern feels that some caregivers do better with some infants than they do with others because of temperamental compatibility—their temperaments match—and that all caregivers do better with all infants if the caregivers try to create an "attunement." For caregivers, attunement can be matching a young child's level of excitement or tone of voice or respectfully leaving an infant alone. Attunement is a feeling felt by the child and the caregiver. The caregiver communicates to the infant, "I have a sense of your feelings, needs, and messages and know the correct next thing to do." When the child senses that other people can and will share in his or her feelings, the child builds a positive sense of self.

Dr. Stern's research carries two powerful messages. The first is that the caregiver's actions with children can always have a positive effect because there are no crucial periods when personality gets set. The second is that, because even little things mean a lot, what caregivers do and how they do it with infants and toddlers are always important.

Overstimulating Babies

If caregivers have a tendency to overstimulate a baby, they should try spending a few minutes imitating the

baby's actions. The practice will slow the caregivers down and will help them read the infant's cues better.

Fostering Toddler Friendships

One of the great advantages of group care for infants and toddlers is the opportunity for early friendships. What a gift it is to have someone to play with who is close to one's size and age and who shares many of the same interests ("Let's climb on that couch!").

Caregivers can promote friendship among young children in their care in many ways. For example:

- Provide enough of similar toys so that infants and toddlers can play together—two toy telephones, plenty of large pop beads, and several buckets and shovels for sand.
- Provide access to large-muscle equipment that two children can use at the same time—a double slide, a big pile of cushions, a hallway in which to cruise back and forth.

Although much of the learning about friendship comes from trial and error, caregivers can help infants and toddlers gain social skills by pointing out apparent feelings, "Jonathan didn't seem to like it when you took his toy," and by encouraging empathy, "Anna seems unhappy because you have the car. Is there another car you could give her to play with?"

Caregivers can also provide a model for friendship by the way they relate to other adults—co-workers, family members, the children's parents. Since no friendship goes smoothly all the time, infants and toddlers will have the opportunity to see how adults deal with differences in a positive way when caregivers demonstrate respect, listening, speaking up, problem-solving, and nurturing in their relationships with other adults.

Understanding Gestures

Hubert Montagner is a French ethologist who has conducted long-term observations of young children in a child care center. He studied gestures, instead of words, sent from child to child. Among other things, he found that by watching how children gesture toward one another, one can predict who will become leaders in the group and who will be popular. He also found that each child spoke to other children through gestures that the other children clearly understood. He found that children fell into patterns of gesturing as early as two years of age, with some using more aggressive gestures and others using more pacifying gestures. One combination of gestures among young children always seemed to draw a friendly response:

> A toddler who tilts his or her head over one shoulder, smiles, and extends one hand toward another child as if to shake hands will usually win the other child over and get what he or she wants from the other child.

Hubert Montagner's research provides insights about early social success and failure. He found that gestural language is easily read by children nine to twelve months of age. Maya Pines, reporting on Hubert Montagner's work in *Psychology Today* (December 1984), lists five types of actions categorized by Dr. Montagner that communicate early social messages. These are:

1. *Actions that pacify others or produce attachment:* offering another child toys or candy, lightly touching or caressing the other child, jumping in place, clapping one's hands, smiling, extending one's hand as if begging, taking the other child's chin in one's hand, cocking one's head over one shoulder, leaning sideways, rocking from left to right, pirouetting or vocalizing in a nonthreatening way.
2. *Threatening actions that generally produce fear, flight or tears in the target child:* loud vocalization, frowning, showing clenched teeth, opening one's mouth wide, pointing one's index finger toward the other child, clenching one's fist, raising one's arm, leaning one's head forward, leaning one's whole trunk forward or shadow boxing.
3. *Aggressive actions:* hitting with hands or feet, scratching, pinching, biting, pulling the other child's hair or clothes, shaking the other child, knocking the other child down, grabbing something that belongs to the other child or throwing something at the other child.
4. *Gestures of fear and retreat:* widening one's eyes, blinking, protecting one's face with bent arms, moving one's head backward, moving one's trunk or one's whole body backward, running away or crying after an encounter with another child.
5. *Actions that produce isolation:* thumb-sucking, tugging at one's hair or ear, sucking on a toy or a blanket, standing or sitting somewhat apart from other children, lying down, lying curled into the fetal position or crying alone.

Dr. Montagner found that children who get others to imitate them and follow them in games show the first type of behaviors (actions that pacify others or produce attachment) as much as the popular children and also give the message, "I do not want to fight but will fight if attacked." Leaders seldom come from children who show the second type of behaviors (threatening actions) because those children are not liked.

Special patterns to watch for include:

- Popular children who never get the preferred toys because they never compete with other children.
- Children who mix signals, for example, offer a toy and kick a leg at the same time. These children are very unpopular.
- Children who mix periods of isolation with sudden acts of aggression, for example, suddenly bite for no reason.

Hubert Montagner believes that the kinds of behaviors that caregivers express can influence the gestural patterns in young children. He noted that certain aggressive patterns changed when the young children's home situation was altered. Caregivers who pay attention to children's gestures and words, give them choices, and are neither overprotective nor aggressive contribute to the development of the first type of behavior in children who, in turn, are either popular or judged as leaders. On the other hand, Dr. Montagner noted that children with dominant-aggressive patterns were usually treated aggressively or with permissiveness by caregivers. The child with a fearful pattern often was overprotected.

It is important to note that all children develop the full range of gestures, types one through five, but how children choose to combine the gestures and how frequently the children choose each type differ greatly. Children with the greatest success at social interactions use many gestures from the pacifying-attaching

category. Children who rely on aggressive actions generally do not form lasting relationships. According to Hubert Montagner, the leaders combine pacifying actions with some attacking sequences, standing their ground with threatening actions when needed.

Sometimes gestures do speak louder than words. Watching for children's gestures helps caregivers better understand their toddlers.

Transmitting Fears

A report published in *Developmental Psychology* in 1985 indicates that twelve-month-old children look to their caregivers to see if they, the children, should or should not fear objects and experiences new to them. In the studies conducted by Joseph Campos and Robert Emde, infants and their mothers were filmed while the children experienced a new task: the children (1) moved toward the mother across Plexiglas suspended 18 inches over a surface; or (2) experienced a new object, an "incredible hulk" doll. Some mothers were instructed to smile and act as though everything was all right and others were to grimace and act as though the situation was dangerous. The children looked to their mothers for advice and showed through their behavior that they took the advice even if they originally had been inclined to act the opposite way toward the action or object.

The research highlights the power of the caregiver to influence the development of fear responses to certain actions and objects. By keeping this knowledge in mind, caregivers can help prevent children from picking up the caregivers' fears.

Caregiver's Practices That Support Social Development

The visions listed here are excerpts from Vision VII in *Visions for Infant/Toddler Care: Guidelines for Professional Caregiving* (see also p. 39 in this guide).

Vision: To develop social skills needed to work and play cooperatively and productively, children must feel secure themselves and value others. While nurturing each child's own self-esteem, caregivers should promote and model interactions that assist children in learning to get along with others and encourage feelings of empathy and mutual respect.

Practices: The infant/toddler caregiver working in a center or family child care home:

- Learns about children's stages of social development and helps children and parents deal with such typical issues as separation anxiety, negative behavior, shyness, sexual identity, and making friends.
- Has realistic expectations for young children's social behavior based on the children's level of development.
- Understands that the social roles and expectations for children in their family setting may be different from the roles and expectations of the child care program and helps the children to behave appropriately in each.
- Encourages children to ask for and accept help from others and to give help to one another.
- Helps children learn to respect the rights and possessions of others.
- Helps the children become aware of their feelings and those of others by talking about feelings with each child.
- Serves as a social model by building a positive relationship with each child and parent and by maintaining positive relationships with other adults in the center or with family members in a family child care home.
- Responds quickly and calmly to prevent children from hurting each other and shows understanding of both aggressor and victim in conflicts.
- Provides individual children with a time-out from social interaction or overstimulation as needed.
- Encourages children to make friends.
- Encourages play and relationships among all children, including children with handicapping conditions and across racial, language, ethnic, age, and gender groups.

Vision: *Young infants* [birth to nine months] enter the world with a capacity and a need for social contact. Infants need both protective and stimulating social interactions with a few familiar, caring adults who get to know the children as individuals; use frequent eye contact; play responsive social games; and talking to the children during feeding, bathing, and dressing. The adults' understanding response to the infants' signals increases the infants' participation in social interactions and their ability to read the signals of others.

Practices: The caregiver working with *young infants:*

- Responds to social gestures and noises of infants and elaborates on the interactions appropriately.
- Plays responsive social games.
- Recognizes that infants need a familiar social partner (caregiver) who is dependable, warm, and loving.
- Takes advantage of opportunities for social play during feeding, bathing, dressing, and other aspects of physical care.

Vision: *Mobile infants* [six to eighteen months] are curious about others but need assistance and supervision in interacting with other children. They continue to need one or a few adults on a consistent basis as their most important social partner(s).

Practices: The caregiver working with *mobile infants:*

- Structures periods of time for social interaction with other children and remains available to protect, comfort, or facilitate but does not interfere unless necessary.
- Provides infants with opportunities to observe social interactions among older children and among adults.
- Provides more than one of several attractive toys to minimize conflicts and waiting for a turn.
- Engages in social play that supports the children's developing social skills, for example, taking turns with a ball, conversing at mealtimes, sharing a snack, putting toys away.
- Encourages children to comfort and help each other.

Vision: *Toddlers'* [sixteen to thirty-six months] social awareness is much more complex than that of younger children. Toddlers can begin to understand that others have feelings, too—sometimes similar to and sometimes different from their own. They imitate many of the social behaviors of other children and adults: taking turns with a ball, sharing a game, putting toys away. As toddlers become increasingly interested in other children, they continue to rely on familiar adults to guide and support their interactions.

Practices: The caregiver working with *toddlers:*

- Encourages cooperation rather than competition.
- Helps toddlers understand that sometimes they must wait for attention because of other children's needs.
- Encourages children to interact with each other in playful and caring ways.
- Understands that sharing, taking turns, and playing with others are difficult for toddlers and encourages their attempts to use words to resolve conflicts.

the Program for infant toddler caregivers

Section Three: Guidance

Introduction

*A*lice S. Honig and Donna S. Wittmer discuss guidance techniques, ways to help the child incorporate within himself or herself the social rules, customs, and values we all live by. The emphasis here is on do's instead of don'ts—that is, guidance not punishment—helping the child learn to get along with others and to accept limits by developing his or her own inner controls.

Alice Honig is a Professor in the Department of Child and Family Studies of Syracuse University's College of Human Development. Dr. Honig teaches various courses, including infancy, theories of child development, preschool models and programs, observation and assessment of infants and young children, and language development. For many years she was the Program Director of the Syracuse University Family Development Research Program, an early intervention with low-income children and families, which was directed by J. Ronald Lally. Dr. Honig was also a member of the intervention program's research staff. Among her many publications are *Infant Caregiving: A Design for Training*, which she coauthored with Dr. Lally, and *Infant/Toddler Caregiving: An Annotated Guide to Media Training Materials,* coauthored with Donna S. Wittmer. Currently, Dr. Honig is a research editor of *Young Children* and conducts numerous training workshops on infant/toddler caregiving around the world.

Donna Wittmer is a Research Assistant Professor for the State University of New York Health Science Center in Syracuse, New York, and directs a grant from the Office of Mental Retardation and Developmental Disabilities of New York State to identify developmental delays and disabilities in a Native American population. She is consultant to the Infant Mental Health Team, Development Evaluation Center, in Syracuse and a Fellow of the National Center for Clinical Infant Programs. She coauthored with Alice S. Honig *Infant/Toddler Caregiving: An Annotated Guide to Media Training Materials* and the *Annotated Bibliography of Discipline*. Dr. Wittmer's article, "Fear in Young Children," was published in *Contemporary Pediatrics* in the spring of 1987.

Guidance: Vision Statement

The caregiver provides a supportive environment in which children can begin to learn and practice appropriate and acceptable behaviors as individuals and as a group.

Knowing what behavior is appropriate or acceptable in a situation is an important skill. Children develop this understanding when consistent limits and realistic expectations of their behavior are clearly and positively defined. Understanding and following simple rules can help children develop self-control. Children feel more secure when they know what is expected of them and when adult expectations realistically take into account each child's development and needs. In nurturing this self-control, caregivers can use a variety of positive guidance methods: listening, reinforcing appropriate behavior, anticipating and defusing conflicts, or redirecting aggression. Negative methods such as spanking, shaming, or threatening can lead to physical and verbal aggression and inhibit the development of self-discipline.

Young infants [birth to nine months] begin to adapt their rhythms of eating and sleeping to the expectations of their social environment through the gentle guidance of sensitive caregivers who meet their needs. Learning basic trust in adults and the environment now makes the child much more open to accepting guidance from adults later on and lays the groundwork for developing self-discipline.

Mobile infants [six to eighteen months] want to do everything, but they have little understanding about what is permissible and cannot remember rules. Adults can organize the environment in ways that clearly define limits and minimize conflicts. While respecting the child's experiments with saying no, caregivers who set appropriate limits can reinforce positive social interaction (e.g., hugging), discourage negative behaviors (e.g., biting), and model how to treat people and things gently.

Toddlers [sixteen to thirty-six months], who move through recurring phases of extreme dependence and independence, gain new skills and awareness. They require an understanding caregiver who remains calm and supportive during their struggle to become independent. Adults must be resourceful in recognizing and encouraging self-reliant behavior (e.g., letting toddlers solve their own problems, when possible, while at the same time setting clear limits).

This statement is an excerpt from Vision VII, Development of Each Child's Competence—Social and Emotional Development, in *Visions for Infant/Toddler Care: Guidelines for Professional Caregiving* (Sacramento: California State Department of Education, 1988). The *Visions* document outlines the visions or goals of The Program for Infant/Toddler Caregivers.

Socialization, Guidance, and Discipline with Infants and Toddlers

Alice S. Honig and Donna S. Wittmer

aying please and thank you, wiping a runny nose on a tissue instead of a sleeve, waiting one's turn, using the toilet properly, asking another child for a toy rather than snatching it, or hitting or biting the other child.

The above learning is called *socialization*—the gradual ways a child incorporates within the self the social rules, customs, and shared values we all live by. But socialization does not happen without help, a special kind of help that patiently fosters a child's willingness to cooperate. Other words for this help are *guidance* and *discipline*.

Our ability as adults to get along with our fellow human beings is rooted in our earliest learning. As soon as children move out of infancy, they start coming to terms with the many different ways society expects them to control impulses, to accept limits, and to understand the reasons for those expectations.

The question is how do you help very young children learn those lessons? What are the best ways? Not all methods work equally well. Sarcasm and slapping, for example, threaten children's self-esteem and hamper healthy emotional growth. Those methods are not good ways to nurture the kinds of responsible future members of society we want. But when discipline is used in a positive way, children feel good about themselves and want to learn social behaviors that make them feel part of the world in which they live.

Discipline is a positive, constructive way of teaching. True discipline is not punishment. Often mistakenly considered the same, the two are profoundly different in approach and results.

Punishment, usually charged with bad feelings, has a negative effect. Spanking, shaming, yelling, criticizing, or locking a child in a closet teaches children to fear you. Punishment may lead to defiance, lying, or sneaking behaviors. Although it sometimes vents an adult's anger, punishment does not teach the social lessons you want the child to learn. For example, when a child is slapped on the hand or given a good shake for turning a television knob or reaching for a simmering pot, the child focuses on the pain and indignity, the feeling of being disliked—*not* on accepting the limits you are trying to teach. Research shows that slapped toddlers rarely remember what they were slapped *for*. (See Chart 4 for a summary of issues related to the use of physical punishment.)

Discipline, on the other hand, teaches compliance by affirming the child's dignity. Discipline focuses on the rule to be learned and the good reasons for the rule, not on the child's "wrongdoing." Instead of arousing feelings of anxiety and rejection, effective discipline supports the child's growing confidence in the world around him or her. The aim is not simply to get the child to comply or to obey rules when you are around to enforce them. The aim is to build the child's inner controls, to develop in the child lifelong habits of governing his or her own behavior.

The purpose of this paper is to examine effective ways you as a caregiver can help guide young children in learning acceptable behavior. The paper will show you how to create the kind of responsive day-to-day environment that helps infants and toddlers grow into adolescents and adults who know how to live by the rules, work together, and respect the rights and needs of others.

Before we discuss particular methods and techniques, however, we need to say a few more words about the roots of socialization and how to approach discipline.

Roots of Socialization

Learning socially acceptable behavior and norms is a long process that starts at an early age. Children learn to cooperate when caregivers provide consistent loving care, guidance, and discipline as well as allow plenty of time for children to learn social skills. (See Chart 5 for a synopsis of the roots of socialization.)

Guidance and Caring Go Together

Cooperation and compliance—the roots of socialization—really begin in infancy. Young infants flourish in a climate of warm, attentive care. By responding to the baby's signals for attention or food or sleep, you are not spoiling the baby. You are meeting the baby's needs and helping the baby learn that the world is a good place to grow up in and that adults can be trusted. Infants whose basic needs for love and care are consistently met are more compliant and cooperative as they grow older than babies whose needs are not met.

Babies can learn to cooperate in a number of ways, such as not crying or fussing when you need to change a wet diaper. But the infants will learn not to fuss only if they truly trust that they will get the bottle or snuggle after changing time. One-year-old babies who are being dressed can hold up an arm helpfully as you start to put on a shirt. Toddlers can learn not to pull the dog's or cat's tail but to pat *gently* as you have suggested and modeled.

The need to instill confidence through affectionate and trusting relationships remains vital as the children grow older. Toddlers are more willing to heed your social rules, to behave as you expect them to, when they feel your basic approval and genuine concern for their well-being.

Guidance Takes Time

Babies need time to absorb and understand what you are trying to teach them. You also need time to teach what you want children to do and how you want them to be.

Infants and toddlers have limited abilities to share with others or to obey rules about avoiding dangerous actions.

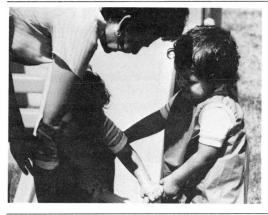

Children need you to *act* to protect them while they learn. Yelling loudly your directions or commands may scare a child or cause him or her to continue a dangerous action more quickly. Instead, move the child or guide the baby away from the problem or help solve the problem. Toddlers need you to restate rules simply, clearly, and meaningfully many, many times. Your planned, thoughtful actions will take time but gradually will be effective.

Prevention Is an Excellent Socialization Tool

Many problems can be avoided if you think ahead. Consider the following example:

One of the caregivers was opening a carton containing a shiny new tricycle. All the toddlers stopped eating and squirmed around at their lunch tables to watch her. "If you don't turn around and eat, you're not going to play with the tricycle," warned the caregiver.

The disciplinary threat was inappropriate. By thinking ahead, by anticipating temptations, disruptions, and sources of conflict, you can prevent unnecessary behavior problems.

Here are some ways to avoid discipline problems:

1. *Child proof the play space.* Make sure no dangerous or breakable materials are within reach so that "no-no" does not have to be a frequent phrase. Wall sockets should be covered and enticing knobs placed out of reach. Do not expect young toddlers to remember safety rules about not running into the street. You must be sure to provide a safe protected place for outdoor play areas. On the other hand, older toddlers can learn to follow the rule to hold on to your hand or a special rope when you take a walk in the neighborhood.

2. *Prepare the play environment thoughtfully.* Allow lots of space for physical activities and large-block play so that toddlers do not easily interfere with each other's building or running. Think about whether your book-reading couch or pillowed corner is too close to where children are allowed to splash with wet, messy materials. Avoid squabbles by providing several of the same kind of toy so that babies can play with the toys while sitting or lying beside each other.

3. *Go over rules ahead of time.* Remind children about rules before activities begin to prevent shoving, fighting, and other misbehavior. Before children go to the sandbox, remind them that sand is for scooping and building. At water playtime you can head off mishaps by reminding toddlers, *before* giving them their plastic basins of water, to keep the water in the basin.

4. *Be consistent.* If you want rules to be effective, be specific about the limits you set and be consistent. If the rule is not to jump on the play mattress until it is empty, or to wash hands before eating, do not slacken or make

exceptions "just this once" because you are in a particular mood or in a hurry.

5. *Vary the tempos of the day.* Plan for enough quieter times after active times. Overexcitement and fatigue lead to troubles. Before coming inside from outdoor play, use calming rituals like whispering games or walking slowly on tiptoes to help the children settle down for naps or storytime. The rhythm of the day can decrease or increase a child's stress. Respond sensitively to the infants' own schedules for sleeping, eating, and playing. Infants and toddlers need long uninterrupted stretches of time to choose their own activities from materials set up in the environment. Chopping up the day and herding children about lead to discipline problems. Toddlers can be offered a group music activity, for example, instead of being forced to stay in a group. Toddlers should have the choice to join a group or not.

6. *Keep promises.* If you promise a toddler the next turn with soap bubbles or a popular toy, be sure to keep your promise. Children who trust your word will work harder at self-control until their turn comes rather than grab the object.

7. *Be aware of individual differences in tolerating stress.* Adrian may have a short temper fuse. Sara cannot sit still for a long story. Juan needs your special help calming down before he can move to indoor play after running about outdoors. Tune in to children's temperaments and personality styles to help prevent some disciplinary problems from arising.

8. *Refocus a toddler's inappropriate actions.* A child about to toddle into mischief often can be redirected to an interesting, safe, and acceptable activity. If you know beforehand that a toddler bites when he or she is

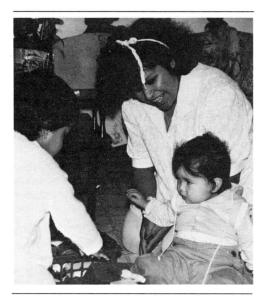

around a certain child, you can refocus the biting child on other activities or keep the child close to you for a while.

9. *Be nearby and attentive.* Babies are not ready to stay out of trouble on their own. They often are unable to distinguish between their own wishes and feelings and those of others. Crawlers cannot curb their natural urge to test, to explore. So infants will need your presence when they are rolling or playing or exploring close to one another. If toddlers are offered messy or wet materials, be present also. Your active presence helps toddlers to remember rules about not dumping water on the floor, for example.

10. *Do not laugh at toddlers.* Laughing *at* a toddler may stop the behavior but can also shame a child. Do not laugh or joke at inappropriate behaviors. Some adults think it is funny or cute if a baby smears potatoes in his or her hair or a toddler says unprintable words. That laughter or joking is guaranteed to increase unwanted behaviors. Calmly ignoring the behavior or calmly restating the rules can help.

Limits Should Be Adapted to Developmental Stages

The basic stages of infants' and toddlers' development are important to understand so you can decide when and how to teach compliance with social rules. Some limits and rules are totally inappropriate for infants and toddlers because the children are not ready for the guidance. For example, infants about one year of age are fascinated with the feel of food. Learning about the squishy texture of food squeezed in fingers may be more important to the infants at that stage than learning a rule to eat only with a spoon and not to "mess" with food.

You will have to choose which rules and limits you emphasize for each child in light of the child's stage of development. Often discipline problems occur because the young child is expected to do something that he or she is not yet

capable of doing. Babies under one year of age, for example, should not have to learn to wait patiently for their nursing. An infant learns a deep basic trust in grown-ups as kind, nurturing, dependable persons when the infant's hunger needs are met promptly. An older toddler, on the other hand, can learn to wait a few minutes until lunch is set down on the table. Yet the toddler may still need your help to wait. Chanting songs together, reassuring the toddler that you are getting the food ready, saying soothing words

that admire how hard the toddler is trying to wait patiently are all discipline techniques that can help toddlers learn patience at mealtimes.

The timing of toilet training also depends on a child's stage of development. Starting toilet learning too early with toddlers can contribute to toddler resistance, anger, or passive acceptance of adult authority. T. Berry Brazelton has found that the *average* age for learning to use the toilet is twenty-seven months. Starting at eighteen months of age is too early for most children. Waiting until the toddler shows interest and signs of readiness makes toilet learning easier for everyone.

Some irksome situations that may require a firmer approach with an older child in care are part of normal toddler development. For example, toddlers like to dart away bravely and without a care as though they are quite self-sufficient. Then, if they are scared they have gone too far, or if they fall and get a bump, or if they grow tired, the toddlers may gallop back and fling themselves passionately at you and demand to be held and reassured or babied. Toddlers typically seesaw between a growing sense of independence and the need to feel that you, the caregiver, are still available and there for them as a "refueling station" when life gets rough. So when some two- or three-year-olds push you away or act "ornery" and changeable, keep in mind that their actions are to be *expected* developmentally and do not require disciplinary teaching.

Sometimes careful judgments are required on your part to decide when a child is ready to learn to comply with certain expectations. Consider the following examples:

1. Early in group care some toddlers may "shadow" you and cling to you. Some suck hard on their thumbs in the new situation and may even refuse to talk or participate much until they begin to feel comfortable

and secure and learn that you are there to love and protect them and to help them learn.

2. A toddler may have great difficulty separating from a parent who must leave for work. The separation anxiety may result in protests, uncooperativeness, withdrawal, or angry reactions.

These situations are not occasions for teaching compliance. They are occasions for understanding, accepting the child's feelings, and building security—making gentle luring attempts to engage the child little by little in objects of interest or by being available to comfort the upset baby.

Socialization Techniques

Before using the suggested techniques, observe the situation carefully and try to figure out what is going on in the child's mind. Are two toddlers touching each other? Observe and let them be unless they are hurting each other. If an infant is taking a toy from another infant, observe. Is the action the start of a friendly give-and-take game between them, or does one baby get very angry and cry? Observe carefully, then use one or more of the techniques when you think intervention is necessary. (See Chart 6 for a synopsis of socialization techniques.)

Change the Environment

Sometimes the environment has to be made richer in order to decrease fights or fusses. When there are enough toys and materials that are truly interesting to the toddlers, the children may grab and push less because they are captivated by the activities. Toddlers are great copycats. When one has a dress-up hat, then two or three others will want to have a hat on too. If one toddler is putting together a pop-bead necklace, there should be enough beads for other children to play with as well.

By contrast, an overly stimulating or noisy environment may cause discipline problems, too. If too many toys lie around in a clutter, you may need to *decrease* the stimulation. Messy, chaotic situations can lead to more jumble and confusion and more occasions of children acting out inappropriately with materials. Arrange to have some toys available and some put out of the way so that disorganized messes and escalating misbehaviors are less likely to occur. Some infants are highly sensitive; they cry more in a noisy environment. They wilt and get very solemn and scared when voice tones are too loud or tense or harsh. Quieting the environment visually and decreasing the noise level usually help the children.

Offer Choices

Toddlers love choices. Decide what choices will be acceptable to you, then offer a toddler, for example, juice or milk, one low-sugar cereal snack or another. When a toddler has difficulty getting settled on the cot for naptime, a back rub and soft songs may help soothe the child, or offering a choice such as "Would you like to sleep with your head at this end of the cot or the other end?" may lead to prompt settling down. The child feels more in control. Toddlers are extremely sensitive to adult pressure, to feeling powerless. Giving children a choice of cot position, clothes for dressing, toys, or activities may avoid confrontations and battles of will. *A balance of power* is created, for example, when you decide what foods to offer a child and the toddler decides how much he or she wants to eat. You decide it is time to go indoors, but the toddlers decide whether they want to walk, push the cart, or be pulled in the wagon as they go inside. When you set up an enriched environment, the child can choose to play with blocks for a few minutes, climb in a box for a while, get a hug from you.

Sometimes giving a choice to a toddler about a specific activity is not appropriate. When a toddler is crabby and rubbing his or her eyes, do not offer a choice of whether to take a nap or not. You decide and help the child firmly and gently into naptime. However, be sure to give the child choices within the limits you have established. In the example of naptime, you can offer to the child choices such as "Do you want to be covered with a blanket?" "Do you want to look at a book?" or "Do you want your favorite teddy bear?"

Help Children with Tantrums

Kicking and howling are not ways for children to get what they want. Toddlers need to learn that tantrums will not work. If toddlers are not hurting themselves or others while they are having a tantrum, "be there" for them. Say, "I know you're angry. I'm here if you need me." Then be there if the child wants a snuggle after the tantrum.

If the child having a tantrum is a danger to himself or herself or to others, hold that child gently but firmly and talk to the child in a soothing steady voice: "I'm not going to let you behave this way. It's not helping you, it's not helping me, it's not going to work. I want you to calm down. When you are calmed down, then you can play. I am holding you to keep you safe."

Focus on "Do's" Instead of "Don'ts"

Focus on "do's" instead of "don'ts." Tell children what you *do* want them to do. "No" and "stop that" are hard words for toddlers to understand, even though they may repeat "No! No!" a lot. They can comply better if they know clearly what is expected or appropriate. Discipline is teaching a child what you would like him or her to do. For example, say:

"Roll the ball on the floor" instead of "Don't throw the ball."

"Hold the baby gently" instead of "Don't squeeze the baby."

"Talk to him, use your words" instead of "Quit hitting."

Rather than say "Don't touch" when a child reaches out to another child, help infants learn what *kinds* of touches are acceptable or comfortable. Use words such as *gently*, *softly*, *slowly*, and *carefully* to help children learn.

For older toddlers a longer explanation may be helpful. Instead of saying, "Don't bother Jackie," try saying:

Jackie is trying to build a tall tower. He is putting one block on top of another carefully so that his tower will get very high. He is worried when you stand very close. He worries that his tower will get bumped and fall down.

Then say:

Would you like to build too? You can build over here in your own space. If you do want to watch Jackie building his tower, here is a safe place to watch from. You can watch just the way we watched when we visited the workmen building at the construction site.

Remind children about rules in a positive way. Ask children to remember or restate a rule rather than scold them. If a toddler is hogging all the playdough at

an art table, ask the child to remember about sharing. What are the rules? Remind the toddler that the playdough needs to stay in the middle of the table so that all the children can reach it. Chant and sing some rules. "Soon we will have to clean up because it is time for lunch" may be easier to remember when chanted in a few familiar notes.

Model Appropriate Behavior

Children learn through imitation, so be a good model for them. Children who are smacked, shouted at, treated harshly, or not listened to will learn to treat others that way. Demonstrate and reinforce through your own daily actions and words the kinds of behavior you want to nourish in children.

Provide Acceptable Alternatives

Offer alternatives to infants who poke or bite or pull hair. A baby may not bite another baby. Biting hurts; a caregiver *cannot* let a child hurt another child. But the baby can bite a teething ring. If a baby wants to pull, you can provide a yarn rope or pull toys or toy furry animals. A toddler may not kick a person, but a child who wants to kick may kick a ball. There are designated places and ways in which some aggressive feelings or urges can be expressed. Hurting others is not one way. Provide alternative objects or materials such as playdough for children to poke and pull and squash.

Appreciate and Encourage Prosocial Behavior

Mature behaviors are built slowly. Accentuate the positive with children. Notice the kind, helpful, and cooperative things they do. Avoid letting undesirable behavior be the best way to get attention. Show appreciation of more acceptable behaviors even when they are only beginnings. Be sure to reward children by praising their efforts to follow rules and treat others fairly. Encourage their *tries.*

It is hard to learn to drink from a cup without spilling or to use the potty without having an accident. Those activities take much practice. Children also need time to learn to pick up toys and put them in a toy box or to use a spoon when eating. (Digging in with both hands will get the food faster to toddlers' mouths.) Give positive personal messages for small steps forward and for small helpful or cooperative actions.

Praise is a way of saying "I like what you did!" The message can be conveyed with a word, a phrase, a gesture, a smile, or a hug. To be effective, the praise must be specific (indicate what you like), immediate, and sincere. Children will feel proud about how hard they are working at more mature behaviors.

Praise builds self-esteem, and as children's self-esteem grows so will their self-control. Your approval will create a glow in a child's heart and eyes. In addition, you will feel more positive about your efforts to socialize the children and discipline them in positive ways.

Share Concerns Firmly About Hurting

Give clear, intense messages that a child must not hurt others. Hold the child firmly and look into the child's eyes. Use "I" statements when you are upset or angry about a child hurting someone. Let the child know where you stand but do not attack the child. Say: "I get upset when you hit. I do not want hitting here. Hitting hurts a person. I am here to protect the children and keep them safe."

Help Children Make Connections

Help children see the connection between what they did to help or hurt another child and how it affected the other child. Say: "You shared your cookie. That made Sharon feel so happy." Or say (intensely): "You bit him. Look, he has bite marks. That really hurt him. He's crying now. See the tears."

Teach Words to Express Strong Emotions

When children can tell you or other children their feelings, they will have less need to act out their anger, fright, or sadness in misbehaviors or uncontrolled crying.

Teach children words to use for feelings. Let children know by your

words that you understand and empathize with the children's upset feelings:

"You are so *hungry*."

"You are so *mad* that Jenny grabbed your toy. You *want* your toy."

"You are *sad* that Shoshy is sick today and is not here to play with you. Shoshy is your friend. You *hope* she feels better soon. You *miss* her."

Teach children to use their words with you and other children. For example, say to a child, "You can tell me, 'I'm angry,'" or "Tell Jenny, 'I want my toy back.'"

Use Hugs and Humor

Hugs and other positive ways of showing affection help children feel happy and secure. Humor is needed often but especially when everything seems to be going wrong. Revise your plan, try to see the humor in the problem, and find ways to salvage the day. Remember, adults are not perfect. They are allowed to make mistakes. Be good to yourself and pat yourself on the back for small steps taken toward your goal of using positive socialization techniques with the children in your care.

Chart Four: The Problem with Physical Punishment

1. Physical punishment is most often a sign of frustration and anger in adults, not a means of teaching children.
2. The use of physical punishment discourages adults from seeking more effective means of teaching children.
3. Physically punished children often do not develop self-control. Adults end up having to act as police officers because as soon as the force is gone, the behavior returns.
4. Physical punishment will frequently increase rather than decrease negative acts. Children who are victims of a lot of physical punishment often tend to be aggressive and hostile. These children frequently become highly resentful, have high levels of mistrust, and display a negative approach toward life and people. Persistent misbehavior is often the only way the children have to communicate that they have unrecognized and unfilled needs.
5. Physical punishment can also result in withdrawn and passive children. Extremely timid people quite typically have a history of much physical punishment.
6. The frequent use of physical punishment is strongly associated with the development of low self-image in children.
7. Physical punishment often results in the permanent cutting off of meaningful communication between the adult and the child.
8. Physical punishment hinders learning and developmental progress. When children are nervous and tense or preoccupied with self-protection, they cannot learn as well or as much as when they are relaxed and alert.
9. Physical punishment does not *teach* children anything at all about constructive ways to resolve conflicts and problems.
10. Physical punishment exposes children to violence, makes children the victims of violence, and provides children with a context for learning violence.

Something to Think About: "Each time I spank I'm teaching, 'when you're angry, hit.' I've never known of a child who was spanked into becoming a more loving human being."—Haim Ginott

Developed by Donna S. Wittmer as a handout for parents.

Chart Five: Roots of Socialization

Guidance and Caring Go Together

Babies whose basic needs for love and care are consistently met are more cooperative as they grow older than babies whose needs are not met.

Guidance Takes Time

Give babies time to absorb and understand what you are trying to teach them.

Prevention Is an Excellent Socialization Tool

1. Child proof the play space.
2. Prepare the play environment thoughtfully.
3. Go over rules ahead of time.
4. Be consistent.
5. Vary the tempos of the day.
6. Keep promises.
7. Be aware of individual differences in tolerating stress.
8. Refocus a toddler's inappropriate actions.
9. Be nearby and attentive.
10. Do not laugh at toddlers.

Limits Should be Adapted to Developmental Stages

You will have to choose which socialization rules you emphasize for each child, depending on the child's stage of development. Often discipline problems occur because the young child is expected to do something that he or she is not yet capable of doing.

Chart Six: Socialization Techniques

Observe the children, read the situation, then act. Some things you might do:

1. *Change the environment.*
   Add more materials *or* reduce the stimulation.

2. *Offer choices.*
   Create a balance of power: Choose the food, then ask, "Do you want milk or juice?"
   You set up the environment—the infant or toddler chooses the activities.

3. *Help children with tantrums.*
   Use the "be there" or "hold and talk" technique to teach children that tantrums or angry outbursts will not work.

4. *Focus on "do's" instead of "don'ts."*
   Focus on "do's" instead of "don'ts." For example, say, "Pat gently" instead of "Don't touch."

5. *Model appropriate behavior.*
   Adults who care for young children should demonstrate the kinds of behavior they want to nourish in children.

6. *Provide acceptable alternatives.*
   Provide alternatives for infants who poke, bite, or hurt another child in any way.

7. *Appreciate and encourage prosocial behavior.*
   Accentuate the positive. Notice the kind, helpful, and cooperative things that children do. Encourage their *tries*.

8. *Share concerns firmly about hurting.*
   Give clear, intense messages that a child must not hurt others, but do not shame or ridicule the child or use physical punishment.

9. *Help children make connections.*
   Help children see the connection between what they did to help or hurt another child and how it affected the other child.

10. *Teach words to express strong emotions.*
    Verbally reflect children's feelings: "You are so angry." Teach children to use their words with you or their peers: "Tell Jenny, 'I want my toy back.' "

11. *Use hugs and humor.*
    Positive affection helps children feel happy and secure. Humor can help you salvage the day.

Practical Tips and Relevant Research

Dealing with Aggressive Behavior

Sometimes caregivers have a difficult time being gentle with an older infant or toddler who is aggressive toward younger ones. An intensely negative reaction toward the aggressor, however, will only increase the child's tension and feelings of insecurity about being lovable. Those feelings, in turn, contribute to aggressive behavior.

The best way to deal with infant or toddler aggression is to prevent incidents from occurring in the first place. When a child in your group has a tendency to sit on or push down others, pull hair, or bite, you need to be even more attentive than usual so that you can move in quickly but

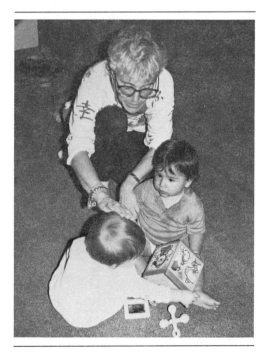

calmly to redirect the aggressor. Sometimes just your being close by will discourage a young toddler's aggressive impulses. Such careful observation and physical proximity will also help you avoid intervening until it is truly necessary.

Remember that an important caregiving goal is to help young children learn social skills, to become more aware of each other's feelings. When a young toddler does hurt or upset a younger infant, both are in need of caring attention. Move close to the two children in a calm way. Comfort the smaller infant, then speak firmly and directly to the older one: "Hilary doesn't like it when you sit on her. See, she is crying." Try to suggest something that will allow the older infant to feel powerful in a constructive way: "If you want to do something *big,* you can carry this big box around. But I'm not going to let you hurt Hilary." If you have ideas ready for a busy toddler bursting with energy, you will be able to focus on meeting the needs of both children.

Considering the Quality of Care

Research published in 1985 by Carollee Howes of the University of California, Los Angeles and Judith Rubenstein of Tufts Medical School shows that caregivers who work shorter hours and have fewer children to care for as well as less responsibility for housework touch, play, and laugh with the children more. Caregivers with opposite situations restrict children more and have children who cry more often. The study also found that stressed caregivers, those who are isolated from other adults or who cope with large numbers of children, are less able to engage in harmonious contacts with the children in their care than caregivers who work in more supportive environments.

When Dr. Howes studied family child care independent of center care, she found that caregivers who work in homes that are specifically designed to be safe and appropriate for children also restrict children less and respond to them more positively. The Howes and Rubenstein research indicates that the conditions under which caregivers work can influence the social and emotional experience of infants and toddlers in their care.

Stephen Suomi takes the importance of quality care one step further in his research with primates published in 1983. He suggests that when the care environment is overcrowded or caregiver or peer behavior is harsh, children with fearful, timid temperaments are particularly at risk because the conditions feed on the children's fear and restrict the children's exploration and movement away from the caregiver.

Taking Objects from an Infant

Infants can get very upset when you take something away from them. One technique that works well is first to show the infant something else that he or she can have. Make sure the infant sees it. The child under fifteen months will almost always reach for the new object. As the child does so, remove the other object from the child's possession and sight. The result is no tears, no protests.

Responding to Competing Demands

Every caregiver has difficult moments when there are more infants in need than there are arms to help, resulting in an unnerving chorus of crying babies. Sometimes those moments can be anticipated, such as at the regular times during the day when most of the children are likely to be hungry or tired. Scheduling extra help at these times can make the routines work much more smoothly.

Even with the best planning, however, trying moments can occur. Rather than panic or blame yourself or race around trying to take care of everyone at once, take a deep breath and proceed calmly. Start by helping the child in greatest distress. Speak comfortingly to the other children, expressing your understanding that they need you, too. Reassure them that you will give them what they need as soon as possible and explain to them how you are helping the child you are with.

Caregiver's Practices That Guide Acceptable Behavior

The visions listed here are excerpts from Vision VII in *Visions for Infant/Toddler Care: Guidelines for Professional Caregiving* (see also p. 63 in this guide).

Vision: Knowing what behavior is appropriate or acceptable in a situation is an important skill. Children develop this understanding when consistent limits and realistic expectations of their behavior are clearly and positively defined. Understanding and following simple rules can help children develop self-control. Children feel more secure when they know what is expected of them and when adult expectations realistically take into account each child's development and needs. In nurturing this self-control, caregivers can use a variety of positive guidance methods: listening, reinforcing appropriate behavior, anticipating and defusing conflicts, or redirecting aggression. Negative methods such as spanking, shaming, or threatening can lead to physical and verbal aggression and inhibit the development of self-discipline.

Practices: The infant/toddler caregiver working in a center or family child care home:

- Builds a trusting relationship with children as a foundation for positive guidance and self-discipline.
- Accepts children's sad or angry feelings, provides acceptable outlets for children to express the feelings, and teaches words for feelings.
- Establishes simple, reasonable, and consistent guidelines, limits, and rules for children's behavior to encourage self-control.
- Alerts children to changes in activities or routines well in advance and handles transitions from one activity to another with clear directions and patience.
- Knows a variety of positive guidance methods—such as listening, reinforcement, and redirection—and uses each appropriately to teach children what to do.
- States directions clearly and positively, for example, says "please walk" instead of "don't run."
- Avoids negative methods such as spanking, threatening, isolating, shaming, or shouting at children.
- Is able to modify play when it becomes overstimulating for any of the children.
- Anticipates confrontations between children and defuses aggressive behavior.
- Addresses the problem behavior or situation rather than labels the child involved, for example, "Oh, the milk spilled, let's clean it up," not "You are so clumsy."
- Helps parents develop realistic expectations for children's behavior in ways that help avoid disciplinary problems, for example, discusses how long children can sit still.
- Encourages parents to talk about child rearing, guidance, and self-discipline and refers the parents to classes, books, and other resources, as appropriate.
- Knows parents' disciplinary methods and expectations and selects those appropriate for use in the center or family child care home.

- Recognizes that serious behavior problems are sometimes related to developmental or emotional problems and works cooperatively with parents toward solutions.
- Is aware of each child's limitations and abilities, uses guidance techniques accordingly, and explains rules at the child's level of understanding.

Vision: *Young infants* [birth to nine months] begin to adapt their rhythms of eating and sleeping to the expectations of their social environment through the gentle guidance of sensitive caregivers who meet their needs. Learning basic trust in adults and the environment now makes the child much more open to accepting guidance from adults later on and lays the groundwork for developing self-discipline.

Practices: The caregiver working with *young infants:*

- Creates an environment of love and trust through warmth and responsive caring.
- Gradually guides infants into regular sleeping and eating patterns but remains responsive to individual needs.
- Responds to infants' needs for comfort and protection.

Vision: *Mobile infants* [six to eighteen months] want to do everything, but they have little understanding about what is permissible and cannot remember rules. Adults can organize the environment in ways that clearly define limits and minimize conflicts. While respecting the child's experiments with saying no, caregivers who set appropriate limits can reinforce positive social interaction (e.g., hugging), discourage negative behaviors (e.g., biting), and model how to treat people and things gently.

Practices: The caregiver working with *mobile infants:*

- Says no when necessary for guidance and safety, moves the child or dangerous object, and gives a simple explanation.
- Has realistic expectations about children's attention spans, interests, social abilities, and physical needs.
- Redirects children gently and explains limits.
- Gives children real choices and accepts the choices made, for example, "Do you want to read a book with me or play on the climber?" or "Shall we have the apples or bananas for snack today?"

Vision: *Toddlers* [sixteen to thirty-six months], who move through recurring phases of extreme dependence and independence, gain new skills and awareness. They require an understanding caregiver who remains calm and supportive during their struggle to become independent. Adults must be resourceful in recognizing and encouraging self-reliant behavior (e.g., letting toddlers solve their own problems, when possible, while at the same time setting clear limits).

Practices: The caregiver working with *toddlers:*

- Lets toddlers solve their own problems whenever possible.
- Limits inappropriate behavior in ways that show respect and support for the toddler's sense of dignity.

- Avoids power struggles by using redirection, distraction, or active listening with toddlers who say no or refuse to cooperate.
- Explains the reasons for limits in simple words, demonstrating whenever possible.
- Uses firm and friendly reminders rather than harsh reprimands when rules are forgotten or disobeyed.
- Uses positive language with children, for example, says "walk" rather than "don't run."
- Follows through on limits set.
- Encourages other adults and older children to use positive guidance and help younger children build self-control.

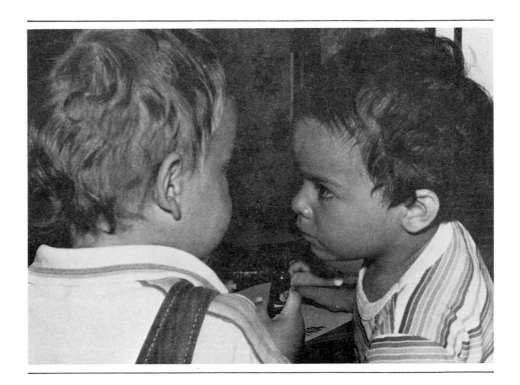

the Program for infant toddler caregivers

Section Four: Appropriate and Inappropriate Practices

Introduction

This section describes appropriate and inappropriate practices related to the social and emotional growth of young children. The practices are written for caregivers and are divided into two parts, one for infants and one for toddlers. In this section *infants* refers to children who are not yet walking and *toddlers* refers to children from the time they begin walking until they are about three years of age.

The majority of practices listed in this section are excerpted from *Developmentally Appropriate Practice*, edited by Sue Bredekamp, copyright 1986 by the National Association for the Education of Young Children (NAEYC); the material is reprinted with the permission of NAEYC. In addition, the descriptions of the final five practices related to toddlers were created especially for this guide.

Appropriate and Inappropriate Practices Related to Infants

In this section infants refers to children who are not yet walking.

Appropriate Practice	*Inappropriate Practice*
• Adults engage in many one-to-one, face-to-face interactions with infants. Adults talk in a pleasant, soothing voice, and use simple language and frequent eye contact.	• Infants are left for long periods in cribs, playpens, or seats without adult attention. Adults are harsh, shout, or use baby talk.
• Infants are held and carried frequently to provide them with a wide variety of experiences. The adults talk to the infant before, during, and after moving the infant around.	• Infants are wordlessly moved about at the adult's convenience. Nothing is explained to infants.
• Adults are especially attentive to infants during routines such as diaper changing, feeding, and changing clothes. The caregiver explains what will happen, what is happening, and what will happen next.	• Routines are swiftly accomplished without involving the infant. Little or no warm interactions take place during routines.
• All interactions are characterized by gentle, supportive responses. Adults listen and respond to sounds that infants make, imitate them, and respect infants' sounds as the beginning of communication.	• Adults are rough, harsh, or ignore the child's responses.
• Caregivers respond quickly to infants' cries or calls of distress, recognizing that crying and body movements are infants' only way to communicate. Responses are soothing and tender.	• Crying is ignored or responded to irregularly at the convenience of the adult. Crying is treated as a nuisance. Adults' responses neglect the infants' needs.
• Playful interactions with babies are done in ways that are sensitive to the child's level of tolerance for physical movement, louder sounds, or other changes.	• Adults frighten, tease, or upset children with their unpredictable behaviors.

Appropriate Practice	*Inappropriate Practice*
• Children's play interests are respected. Adults observe the child's activity and comment, offer additional ideas for play, and encourage the child's engagement in the activity.	• Infants are interrupted, toys are whisked from their grasp, adults impose their own ideas or even play with toys themselves regardless of the child's interest.
• The caregiver frequently talks with, sings to, and reads to infants. Language is a vital, lively form of communication with individuals.	• Infants are expected to entertain themselves or watch television. Language is used infrequently and vocabularies [are] limited.
• Infants and their parents are greeted warmly and with enthusiasm each morning. The caregiver holds the baby upon arrival and gradually helps the child become a part of the small group.	• Babies are placed on the floor or in a crib with no caregiver interaction. Caregivers receive children coldly and without individual attention.
• Caregivers consistently respond to infants' needs for food and comfort thus enabling the infants to develop trust in the adults who care for them, so they find the world a secure place to be.	• Adults are unpredictable and/or unresponsive. They act as if children are a bother.
• Caregivers adjust to infants' individual feeding and sleeping schedules. Their food preferences and eating styles are respected.	• Schedules are rigid and based on adults' rather than children's needs. Food is used for rewards (or denied as punishment).
• Infants are praised for their accomplishments and helped to feel increasingly competent.	• Infants are criticized for what they cannot do or for their clumsy struggle to master a skill. They are made to feel inadequate and that they have no effect on others.
• Teachers [caregivers] respect infants' curiosity about each other. At the same time, adults help ensure that children treat each other gently.	• Infants are not allowed to touch each other gently, or are forced to share or play together when they have no interest in doing so.
• Adults model the type of interactions with others that they want children to develop.	• Adults are aggressive, shout, or exhibit a lack of coping behaviors under stress.
• Adults frequently engage in games such as Peek-a-Boo and 5 Little Piggies with infants who are interested and responsive to the play.	• Games are imposed on children regardless of their interest. Play is seen as a time filler rather than a learning experience.

Appropriate Practice	*Inappropriate Practice*
• Diaper changing, feeding, and other routines are viewed as vital learning experiences for babies.	• Routines are dealt with superficially and indifferently.
• Healthy, accepting attitudes about children's bodies and their functions are expressed.	• Infants are made to feel their bodies are not to be touched or admired, and that bodily functions are disgusting.

Appropriate and Inappropriate Practices Related to Toddlers

In this section toddlers refers to children from the time they begin walking until they are about three years of age.

Appropriate Practice	*Inappropriate Practice*
• Adults engage in many one-to-one, face-to-face conversations with toddlers. Adults let toddlers initiate language, and wait for a response, even from children whose language is limited. Adults label or name objects, describe events, and reflect feelings to help children learn new words. Adults simplify their language for toddlers who are just beginning to talk (instead of "It's time to wash our hands and have a snack," the adult says, "Let's wash hands. Snacktime!"). Then as children acquire their own words, adults expand on the toddler's language (for example, *Toddler*—"Mary sock." *Adult*—"Oh, that's Mary's missing sock and you found it.").	• Adults talk *at* toddlers and do not wait for a response. Adult voices dominate or adults do not speak to children because they think they are too young to respond. Adults either talk "baby talk" or use language that is too complex for toddlers to understand.
• Adults are supportive of toddlers as they acquire skills. Adults watch to see what the child is trying to do and provide the necessary support to help the child accomplish the task, allowing children to do what they are capable of doing and assisting with tasks that are frustrating.	• Adults are impatient and intrusive. They expect too much or too little of toddlers. Because it is faster, adults do tasks for toddlers that children can do themselves. Or adults allow children to become frustrated by tasks they cannot do.
• Adults respond quickly to toddlers' cries or calls for help, recognizing that toddlers have limited language with which to communicate their needs.	• Crying is ignored or responded to irregularly or at the adults' convenience.

Appropriate Practice	*Inappropriate Practice*
• Adults respect children's developing preferences for familiar objects, foods, and people. Adults permit children to keep their own favorite objects and provide limited options from which children may choose what they prefer to eat or wear. Children's preferences are seen as a healthy indication of a developing self-concept.	• Adults prohibit favored objects like blankets or toys or arbitrarily take them away or expect toddlers to share them with other children. Children are not given choices and preferences are not encouraged. Children are all expected to do the same thing.
• Adults respect toddlers' desire to carry favored objects around with them, to move objects like household items from one place to another, and to roam around or sit and parallel play with toys and objects.	• Adults restrict objects to certain locations and do not tolerate hoarding, collecting, or carrying.
• Adults patiently redirect toddlers to help guide children toward controlling their own impulses and behavior. When children fight over the same toy, the adult provides another like it or removes the toy. If neither of these strategies is effective, the adult may gently remove the toddler and redirect the child's attention by initiating play in another area. Adults only punish children for overtly dangerous behavior.	• Adults ignore disputes leading to a chaotic atmosphere or punish infractions harshly, frightening and humiliating children.
• Adults recognize that constantly testing limits and expressing opposition to adults ("NO!") is part of developing a healthy sense of self as a separate, autonomous individual. Adults only say "No" when the prohibition relates to children's safety. Adults give positively worded directions ("Bang on the floor") not just restrictions ("Don't bang on the table").	• Adults are constantly saying "No!" to toddlers or becoming involved in power struggles over issues that do not relate to the child's health or well-being. Adults punish children for asserting themselves or saying "No."
• Children are praised for their accomplishments and helped to feel increasingly competent and in control of themselves.	• Toddlers are criticized for what they cannot do or for their clumsy struggle to master a skill. Or adults foster dependency; children are overprotected and made to feel inadequate.

Appropriate Practice	*Inappropriate Practice*
• Children and their parents are greeted warmly and with enthusiasm each morning. The day begins with a great deal of adult–child contact. Adults help toddlers settle into the group by reading books or quietly playing with them.	• Children are received coldly and given no individual attention. Toddlers are expected to begin the day with free play and little adult supervision.
• Adults model the type of interactions with others that they want children to develop. Adults recognize that most of the time when toddlers are aggressive, hurting or biting other children, it is because they lack skills to cope with frustrating situations such as wanting another child's toy. Adults model for toddlers the words to say ("Susan, I want the jack-in-the-box now") or redirect them to another activity.	• Adults are aggressive, shout, or exhibit a lack of coping behaviors under stress. Adult attempts to punish or control the aggressive toddler escalate the hostility.
• Caregivers are sensitive to differing cultural expectations concerning a toddler's emerging independence and expressions of feelings. Caregivers are supportive of children who are learning two languages.	• All children are treated the same regardless of cultural and language differences.
• Caregivers assist toddlers in recognizing and accepting their feelings, such as joy, jealousy, fear, affection, anger. Children are encouraged to express feelings in appropriate ways.	• Children are punished or shamed for having or expressing "negative" feelings such as anger, fear, or sadness.
• Caregivers are sensitive to children's needs for attention and affection and respond to those needs.	• Food is used to pacify children and as a substitute for the caregiver's attention.
• Caregivers support family relationships by talking about the child's family members, where they are, what they are doing, when they will be back. Caregivers use books, stories, and discussions to help children with special life and family experiences, such as divorce, moving, or birth of a sibling.	• Caregivers make no attempt to include the child's family or life situation into the child's experiences at child care.
• Caregivers encourage cooperation by being close by as children take turns with a toy, share a snack, put away toys. Caregivers understand that waiting, taking turns, and sharing are difficult for toddlers; caregivers support all such efforts, however small.	• Caregivers are casual about supervising toddlers engaged in potentially difficult situations; caregivers do not anticipate potential problems and resort to negative methods, such as shouting and spanking or isolating children.

the Program for infant toddler caregivers

Section Five: Suggested Resources

Suggested Resources

Books and Articles

Beginnings: The Social and Affective Development of Black Children. Edited by Margaret B. Spencer and others. Hillsdale, N.J.: Lawrence Erlbaum Associates, Inc., 1985.

Offers important approaches to the understanding and study of the development of minority children, although none of the chapters deals specifically with infancy.

Brazelton, T. Berry. *Infants and Mothers: Differences in Development* (Revised edition). New York: Delacorte Press, 1983.

Describes three different types of babies—active, average, and quiet—to illustrate how temperamental differences influence the lives and care of infants.

Brazelton, T. Berry, and Michael E. Yogman. *Affective Development in Infancy.* Norwood, N.J.: Ablex Publishing Corporation, 1986.

Gives an overview of emotional development in infants, with chapters contributed by experts from the fields of pediatrics, child development, psychology, psychiatry, and psychoanalysis. Topics covered include the transfer of feelings from caregiver to infant, attachment, and the impact of switching child care settings on infants and toddlers.

Chess, Stella, and Alexander Thomas. *Know Your Child: An Authoritative Guide for Today's Parents.* New York: Basic Books, Inc., 1987.

Provides a detailed description of the different temperamental traits identified in Alexander Thomas's and Stella Chess's research. Indicates how parents (and other caregivers) can use knowledge about temperament to adapt to individual children.

Chess, Stella, and Mahin Hassibi. *Principles and Practice of Child Psychiatry* (Second edition). New York: Plenum Publishing Corp., 1986.

Cutrona, Carolyn E., and Beth R. Troutman. "Social Support, Infant Temperament, and Parenting Self-Efficacy: A Mediational Model of Postpartum Depression," *Child Development*, Vol. 57 (December, 1986), 1,507–1,518.

Reports on research that found mothers with temperamentally difficult infants experience depression because they cannot comfort their infants. Carolyn Cutrona and Beth Troutman suggest that mothers with difficult infants need a network of support to help them cope with the stress. Caregivers may want to use such an approach when they experience the stress of caring for a difficult infant.

Developmentally Appropriate Practice in Early Childhood Programs Serving Children From Birth Through Age 8 (Expanded edition). Edited by Sue Bredekamp. Washington, D.C.: National Association for the Education of Young Children, 1988.

Presents NAEYC's position statement on developmentally appropriate practice in early childhood programs serving children from birth to age eight years. Lists appropriate and inappropriate practices.

Erikson, Erik H. *Childhood and Society* (Thirty-fifth anniversary edition). New York: W.W. Norton & Company, Inc., 1986.

Presents Erik Erikson's theory of ego development. Eight critical developmental periods are defined. Through clinical descriptions the author explains how the issues of basic trust versus mistrust and autonomy versus shame and doubt are critical during infancy.

Fraiberg, Selma H. *The Magic Years: Understanding and Handling the Problems of Early Childhood*. New York: Charles Scribner's Sons, 1984.

A classic on how the caregiver's day-to-day contact with an infant influences emotional development and feelings of security. Written from a psychoanalytic perspective, the book offers practical information on how caregivers can better understand messages from babies and engage in a truly reciprocal relationship with them.

Gerber, Magda. "Caring for Infants with Respect: The RIE Approach," *Zero to Three* (February, 1984), 1-3.

Presents Magda Gerber's approach to caring for infants and toddlers. She recommends that caregivers always respect babies, whatever their emotional state.

Greenspan, Stanley, and Nancy T. Greenspan. *First Feelings: Milestones in the Emotional Development of Your Baby and Child from Birth to Age Four*. New York: Viking Penguin, Inc., 1985.

Defines emotional milestones during infancy and early childhood and offers guidelines for active caregiving.

Greenspan, Stanley I. *The Clinical Interview of the Child: Theory and Practice*. New York: McGraw-Hill Book Co., 1981.

Greenspan, Stanley I. *Intelligence and Adaptation*. Madison, Conn.: International Universities Press, Inc., 1980.

Explores the relationship between emotional and cognitive or intellectual development during infancy within a unified framework. Particular emphasis is given to the psychoanalytic model and Jean Piaget's model of early development.

Greenspan, Stanley I. *Psychopathology and Adaptation in Infancy and Early Childhood*. Madison, Conn.: International Universities Press, Inc., 1983.

Honig, Alice Sterling. "Research in Review: Compliance, Control, and Discipline," *Young Children*, Vol. 40 (January, 1985), 50-58; (March, 1985), 47-52.

Reviews research on different discipline techniques that affect young children's compliance, self-esteem, and self-control.

Honig, Alice S., and J. Ronald Lally. *Infant Caregiving: A Design for Training*. Syracuse, N.Y.: Syracuse University Press, 1981.

A handbook for trainers that focuses on the group care of children from birth to age three years.

Howes, Carollee, and Judith L. Rubenstein. "Determinants of Toddlers' Experience in Day Care: Age of Entry and Quality of Setting," *Child Care Quarterly*, Vol. 14 (1985), 140-151.

Shows how the conditions under which caregivers work influence the social and emotional experience of infants and toddlers.

Infants in Multirisk Families: Case Studies in Preventive Intervention. Edited by Stanley I. Greenspan. Madison, Conn.: International Universities Press, Inc., 1987.

Kagan, Jerome. *The Nature of the Child.* New York: Basic Books, Inc., 1984.

Presents an overview of different temperaments of infants and toddlers. A particular emphasis is given to cautious behavior, which appears very early in some infants and persists as they grow older.

Kaplan, Louise J. *Oneness and Separateness.* New York: Simon & Schuster, Inc., 1978.

Uses Margaret Mahler's theory and clinical insight to examine infant personality. Infants are described as having both an urge for oneness with the caregiver and an opposing urge to become a separate self.

Lally, J. Ronald, and Ira Gordon. *Learning Games for Infants and Toddlers.* Syracuse, N.Y.: New Readers Press, 1977.

Oster, H. "Facial Expressions and Affect Development," in *The Development of Affect.* Edited by M. Lewis and L.A. Rosenblum. New York: Plenum Publishing Corp., 1978.

Examines the development and meaning of facial expressions in young children.

Pines, Maya. "Children's Winning Ways," *Psychology Today*, Vol. 12 (December, 1984), 58-65.

Summarizes the work of ethologist Hubert Montagner, who has studied the gestural language of children. A key finding of Dr. Montagner's is how some children as early as two years of age use more aggressive gestures and other children use more pacifying gestures.

Sorce, J.F., Robert N. Emde, Joseph Campos, and M.D. Klinnert. "Maternal Emotional Signaling: Its Effect on the Visual Cliff Behavior of One-year-olds," *Developmental Psychology*, Vol. 21 (1985), 195-200.

Summarizes a study which is part of the ongoing work of Robert Emde and Joseph Campos on the transmission of emotions from caregivers to infants. The experiment shows how adults communicate fear and security to infants.

Sroufe, Alan. *Knowing and Enjoying Your Baby.* Englewood Cliffs, N.J.: Prentice Hall, 1977.

Describes the expression and development of emotions in infants, including joy, smiles, laughter, and fear of the unfamiliar. Caregivers can use this information to become more keenly aware of babies' emotional messages.

Stern, Daniel N. *The Interpersonal World of the Infant: A View from Psychoanalysis and Developmental Psychology.* New York: Basic Books, Inc., 1985.

Presents the view that children's personalities are influenced more by day-to-day encounters with caregivers than by "critical periods" of development. Attunement between the caregiver and each infant is considered essential. For example, caregivers who match infants' level of excitement or tone of voice communicate that other people understand and share the infants' feelings.

Suomi, Stephen J. "Social Development in Rhesus Monkeys: Consideration of Individual Differences," in *The Behavior of Human Infants*. Edited by A. Oliverio and M. Zappella. New York: Plenum Publishing Corp., 1983.

Reviews research with young primates that shows how factors such as over-crowding or restrictive caregiving related to the quality of care are particularly harmful to fearful or timid infants. This work underscores the importance of being aware of individual differences in infants and toddlers and shows how each child reacts differently to different caregiving arrangements.

Thoman, Evelyn B., and Sue Browder. *Born Dancing: The Relaxed Parents' Guide to Making Babies Smart with Love*. New York: Harper & Row Pubs., Inc., 1987.

Explores how babies communicate their feelings with gestures, eye movements, and sounds. Describes how caregivers can trust, respect, and understand babies' unspoken language and natural rhythms and engage in a dance with the babies.

Thomas, Alexander, Stella Chess, and others. *Behavioral Individuality in Early Childhood*. Westport, Conn.: Greenwood Press, Inc., 1980.

Audiovisuals

Babies Are People, Too. Los Angeles: Churchill Films, 1985. Videocassette, color, 27 minutes.

Focuses on the relationship between young mothers and their children during the first two years of life.

Addresses the difficulties young mothers have in coping with the simultaneous tasks of adolescence and parenting. Theoretical concepts (e.g., bonding, attachment behaviors, separation/individuation, and autono-mous/oppositional behaviors) are presented in language that is easy to understand. The film also shows positive discipline techniques for smoother transitions from child care at the end of the day.

Available from Churchill Films, 662 North Robertson Blvd., Los Angeles, CA 90069-9990; telephone (213) 657-5110, (800) 334-7830.

Day to Day with Your Child (Program 2): *The Infant's Communication*. Mount Kisco, N.Y.: Guidance Associates, 1977. Filmstrip/sound cassette and filmstrip on video, color, 34 minutes total (five programs).

Illustrates how caregivers can learn to recognize cries of fear, hunger, and discomfort. Feeding, dressing, and diapering are discussed as good times for caregivers to talk with babies and to comment on what they are doing. Excellent pictures show caregivers talking to a baby face to face.

Stranger anxiety is discussed, including advice for parents on the impor-tance of accepting their babies' fear of strangers.

Available from Guidance Associates, Communications Park, Box 3000, Mount Kisco, NY 10549; telephone (914) 666-4100, (800) 431-1242.

Day to Day with Your Child (Program 5): *Discipline—What Is It?* Mount Kisco, N.Y.: Guidance Associates, 1977. Filmstrip/sound cassette and filmstrip on video, color, 34 minutes total (five programs).

Demonstrates positive discipline techniques. As the guide states: "Good discipline is a partnership between children and the adults in their lives. It is not the same as punishment. Rather, it is the way in which youngsters learn self-control and responsibility for their behavior. As a result of good discipline, children learn that they can handle themselves and get along with others."

Available from Guidance Associates, Communications Park, Box 3000, Mount Kisco, NY 10549; telephone (914) 666-4100, (800) 431-1242.

First Moves: Welcoming a Child to a New Caregiving Setting. Sacramento: California State Department of Education, 1986. Videocassette, color, 26 minutes.

Presents practical techniques caregivers can use to introduce young children to a new care setting and ease difficult separations between parent and child. The transition from parent to new caregiver goes more smoothly when the caregiver (1) keeps an initial distance from the child, ensuring enough space for the child to size things up; (2) makes contact indirectly through some interesting object; and (3) allows time for the transition to occur.

The video also stresses the value of get-acquainted visits before the first day, the importance of involving the parent as a partner in the separation process, and the need to adapt these techniques to children at different developmental stages.

Flexible, Fearful, or Feisty: The Different Temperaments of Infants and Toddlers. Sacramento: California State Department of Education, 1990. Videocassette, color, 29 minutes.

Explores various temperamental styles of infants and toddlers. Provides caregivers with techniques for dealing with the differences between individual infants and toddlers in group child care settings.

Getting in Tune: Creating Nurturing Relationships with Infants and Toddlers. Sacramento: California State Department of Education, 1990. Videocassette, color, 24 minutes.

Presents steps caregivers can take to establish supportive, responsive relationships with infants and toddlers. The video stresses the importance of early emotional support and describes how caregivers can provide that support. The "responsive process" is presented; the process includes three steps—watching, asking, and adapting—to help a caregiver learn what a young child needs and how best to react to that need. Shows how caregivers can recognize the parts of their own personality that might hinder their ability to get in tune with certain children.

Human Development: A New Look at the Infant (Program 5): *Attachment.* Irvine, Calif.: Concept Media, 1983. Videocassette and filmstrip/sound cassette, color, 27 minutes.

Reviews Mary Ainsworth's work in the area of attachment. Discusses attachment behaviors and the roles they play in separations and reunions. Explores the importance of caregiver sensitivity.

Available from Concept Media, P.O. Box 19542, Irvine, CA 92713-9542.

It's Not Just Routine: Feeding, Diapering, and Napping Infants and Toddlers. Sacramento: California State Department of Education, 1990. Videocassette, color, 24 minutes.

Addresses the need for caregivers to use feeding, napping, and diapering routines as opportunities to build a close personal relationship with each child while attending to the child's physical, emotional, and other developmental needs.

Life's First Feelings. Deerfield, Ill.: Coronet Films and Video, 1985. Videocassette, color, 50 minutes.

Explores infants' and toddlers' rich social and emotional lives (first feelings) through interviews with various experts in the field. Topics include some babies' oversensitivity to sight, sound, or touch and how to handle such babies; sibling rivalry and how to build self-esteem in the older child; facial expressions as a window into the child's emotional state; temperamental differences in young children; the influence of social factors on children's behavior as babies get older; parenting behaviors that encourage caring behaviors in young children; and the baby's responsiveness to the parent's facial expressions.

Available from Coronet Films and Video (WGBH Education Foundation), 108 Wilnot Rd., Deerfield, IL 60015; telephone (800) 621-2131.

Nurturing. Belmont, Calif.: Davidson Films, Inc., [n.d.]. Videocassette, color, 17 minutes.

Illustrates how thoughtful infant care practices boost the emotional and mental growth of babies. Stranger anxiety is beautifully presented as a normal stage of infant development. The need for careful transitions is stressed to give infants a chance to become acquainted with new adult caregivers. Fathers are also shown as caregivers who converse with the baby and support the baby's safe exploration of a living-room environment.

Available from Davidson Films, Inc., 850 O'Neill Avenue, Belmont, CA 94002; telephone (415) 591-8319.

The Psychological Birth of the Human Infant. Franklin Lakes, N.J.: Mahler Research Foundation Film Library, 1985. Videocassette, black and white, 50 minutes.

Shows footage from the original research data of Dr. Margaret S. Mahler and her co-workers. Dr. Mahler introduces and narrates the film, demonstrating the stages through which infants progress in their relationships with their mothers. The academic style of presentation in this film requires that a trainer be present when the film is shown to caregivers. The film is excellent for teaching trainers about the "psychological birth" of an infant and will help trainers assist caregivers in understanding the struggles of infants as they move toward greater independence.

Available from Mahler Research Foundation Film Library, P.O. Box 315, Franklin Lakes, NJ 07417; telephone (201) 891-8240.

For information on most of the videos and filmstrips/cassettes listed here, see *Infant/Toddler Caregiving: An Annotated Guide to Media Training Materials* (Sacramento: California Department of Education, 1988). To order California Department of Education materials, see Ordering Information on page ii of this guide.

Publications Available from the Department of Education

This publication is a component of The Program for Infant/Toddler Caregivers that is available from the California Department of Education. Other titles in The Program are the following:

Item No.	Title (Date of publication)	Price
0883	The Ages of Infancy: Caring for Young, Mobile, and Older Infants (videocassette and guide) (1990)*	$65.00
1045	Discoveries of Infancy: Cognitive Development and Learning (videocassette and guide) (1992)*	65.00
1056	Essential Connections: Ten Keys to Culturally Sensitive Care (videocassette and guide) (1993)*	65.00
0751	First Moves: Welcoming a Child to a New Caregiving Setting (videocassette and guide) (1988)*	65.00
0839	Flexible, Fearful, or Feisty: The Different Temperaments of Infants and Toddlers (videocassette and guide) (1990)*	65.00
0809	Getting In Tune: Creating Nurturing Relationships with Infants and Toddlers (videocassette and guide) (1990)*	65.00
0750	Infant/Toddler Caregiving: An Annotated Guide to Media Training Materials (1989)	9.50
0878	Infant/Toddler Caregiving: A Guide to Creating Partnerships with Parents (1990)	10.00
0880	Infant/Toddler Caregiving: A Guide to Language Development and Communication (1990)	10.00
0877	Infant/Toddler Caregiving: A Guide to Routines (1990)	10.00
0879	Infant/Toddler Caregiving: A Guide to Setting Up Environments (1990)	10.00
0876	Infant/Toddler Caregiving: A Guide to Social–Emotional Growth and Socialization (1990)	10.00
0869	It's Not Just Routine: Feeding, Diapering, and Napping Infants and Toddlers (videocassette and guide) (1990)*	65.00
0753	Respectfully Yours: Magda Gerber's Approach to Professional Infant/Toddler Care (videocassette and guide) (1988)*	65.00
1042	School Nutrition Facility Planning Guide (1992)	8.00
0752	Space to Grow: Creating a Child Care Environment for Infants and Toddlers (videocassette and guide) (1988)*	65.00
1044	Together in Care: Meeting the Intimacy Needs of Infants and Toddlers in Groups (videocassette and guide) (1992)*	65.00
0758	Visions for Infant/Toddler Care: Guidelines for Professional Caregiving (1989)	6.50

*Videocassette also available in Chinese (Cantonese) and Spanish at the same price.

Orders should be directed to:

California Department of Education
P.O. Box 271
Sacramento, CA 95812-0271

Please include the item number for each title ordered.

Remittance or purchase order must accompany order. Purchase orders without checks are accepted only from governmental agencies. Sales tax should be added to all orders from California purchasers. Stated prices, which include shipping charges to anywhere in the United States, are subject to change.

A complete list of publications available from the Department, including apprenticeship instructional materials, may be obtained by writing to the address listed above or by calling (916) 445-1260.

93 84073   R92-121 (Second printing) 84073 003-0175B 11-93